LOCOMOTION PAPERS

GW00536538

The
MELBOURNE MILITARY RAILWAY

A History of the Railway Training Centre at Melbourne and King's Newton: 1939–1945

by
Alan Cooper, Peter Leggott
Cyril Sprenger

THE OAKWOOD PRESS

© Oakwood Press 1990

ISBN 0 85361 411 3

Typeset by Gem Publishing Company, Brightwell, Wallingford, Oxfordshire.

Printed by Alphaprint, Witney, Oxfordshire.

Acknowledgements

The authors' thanks are due to many people who have helped in various ways in the production of this book. It is not possible to mention them *all* by name, but we must mention the following:

Syd Arkell	Harry R. McLaughlin
Ted Baller	Stephen Percival
Jim Brennan	Colin Pomeroy (The Colonel)
Bernard Cloake	Jim Roberts
Sam Ernill	Ken Smethurst
G.R.T. Evans	Howard Sprenger
George Grouch	Dennis Spencer
Clive Hardy	I.G. Tarrant (ex-CSM)
Ken Hicklin	Glynn Waite
A.P. Lambert	George Williams
Henry Libby (USA)	Godfrey Yeomans

We thank all those who supplied photographs, and owe a debt of gratitude to the following organisations:

The Canadian High Commission
The Curator and Staff of the Museum of Military Transport, Beverley
The *Derby Evening Telegraph*
The Derbyshire County Library, Matlock (via Ray Rippingale)
The Public Record Office at Kew
The United States of America Embassy
The Archive Section of the United States Department of Defense.

Our wives have been duly thanked elsewhere in the book, but our final acknowledgement goes to those who gave us encouragement when we thought that the whole thing would never, ever be published.

AC, PL and CS, 1990

Published by
The OAKWOOD PRESS
P.O.Box 122, Headington, Oxford.

Contents

The northern end of the 308 yds-long Ashby tunnel.   *R.C. Riley Collection*

RAILWAY STATION, MELBOURNE.

E. MARTIN.

R.J. Essery Collection

A fine postcard view of Melbourne station in Midland days.

Foreword

This book, like many others perhaps, began in a chat in a pub. In 1979 Clive Hardy and Russ Brown wrote a book about *Derby at War*, and Cyril Sprenger contributed a Foreword to it. Shortly after its publication the three of us and Clive Hardy were discussing the book, and the conversation turned to the Melbourne Military Railway. None of us knew of any general account of the line, and this book grew from there, the pattern of it being ultimately determined by the material we have managed to collect. We have extended the scope of the book to include some description of the Longmoor Military Railway as Melbourne was a satellite of that military railway training centre.

In 1974 D.W. Ronald and R.J. Carter wrote a general history of the Longmoor Military Railway, and we have not attempted to re-iterate their detailed account of the war years 1939–1945. There was also, of course, the Official History of the Corps of Royal Engineers, and R. Tourret has written the two-volume *Allied Military Locomotives of the Second World War*, all of which are necessary reading for anyone interested in our subject. We have tried to give as detailed an account as possible, but to include the human history of the training centres, too. We also thought that it would be interesting to find out what the RE railwaymen did in their service overseas. They told us – and we have deleted most of the expletives!

Since American and Canadian railroad men came to Longmoor and Melbourne to learn about operating conditions in Britain and Europe, we have included accounts of their activities, too. We have not tried to write about every American or Canadian unit, but about those known to have had significant connections with the two training centres.

We have searched for official records wherever possible, but our search has not been very fruitful. We are, however, grateful to regimental archivists and museum curators who have searched diligently on our behalf, and in particular we must thank the most helpful staff of the Public Record Office at Kew, and of the Museum of Army Transport at Beverley. We record elsewhere our thanks to all those who have helped us to trace records, or who have contributed their memories and, in many cases, photographs, but we must acknowledge our debt to all those who have taken the time to write to us, to talk to us on the telephone, or to meet us to discuss the war years.

Our researches have involved us in some fascinating visits, and brought us much interesting correspondence. We must here thank our wives for their patience with our fanaticism, and for believing us whenever we said that we had to visit a pub 'to see a man about the book'. As a result of all this we have made many new friends. We have not written THE history of Railway Training Centres, but we have tried to write a history which has recorded proper justice to all those who have helped us. Any errors in the account are, of course, entirely our own.

August 1990

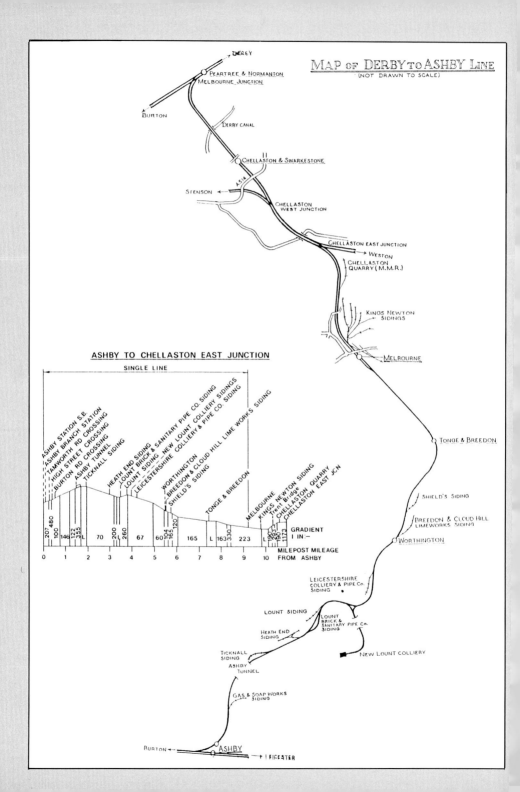

Chapter One
'In the Mood'
(Railways in Warfare)

An efficient transport system has always been vital to the successful conduct of warfare. The network of Roman roads across their Empire is testament to their recognition of this need, and to their engineering skill in meeting it. In Britain in the 18th century the Scottish Highlands owed their subjugation probably more to the road construction of General Wade's engineers than to 'Butcher' Cumberland and his cavalry. General Wade is indeed a rare figure – a military engineer known to popular history.

Until the nineteenth century military transport meant the building of roads or, for Britain, a search for ways of hitting an enemy where the Royal Navy could provide both fighting power and transportation. So, Britain fought the French in a long series of wars in Spain, Canada and India, and the Russians in the Crimea. That policy did not change and certainly contributed to strategic thinking in both great wars of this century, but during the nineteenth century Britain led the world in the development of a new form of transport – the railway. Railways had so much to offer in developing transportation that they quickly spread to Europe and North America, and British engineers and navvies took a leading role in this spread of the railways. Little regard was paid to railways by military strategists, despite an early example of their value in rapid movement of troops in the transfer of the Guards from London to Manchester to help quell civil disorder in 1835. A further demonstration of the possible value of railways in military supply was given in 1855 when the railway contractors Peto, Betts and Brassey assembled a force of navvies, sailed to Balaklava and built a supply line from the harbour to the British forces besieging Sebastopol. This railway transformed the supply position, and could have done much more had it been properly utilised.

The military planners in France and, to a greater degree, those of Prussia saw the strategic value of railways and contributed largely to the pattern of railway construction in their countries. The Prussians in particular reaped military rewards from this in the rapid movement of troops in their 'lightning wars' (or *blitzkriegs*) against Denmark in 1865, Austria in 1866 and France in 1870. Indeed, it has been suggested that German railway timetables were the factor which made war inevitable after mobilisation in 1914. The Civil War in the United States of America also showed the value of railway transportation in warfare. The North had a much more extensive railway system than the South, being much more industrialised, but they also made more effective use of what they had. American ingenuity, often crucial in World War II, showed itself in the Civil War in the development of armoured trains and the use of observation balloons towed by locomotives. The failure of Confederate forces to cut effectively the single line of track supplying his forces, made possible the great 'march through the South' of General Sherman which broke the Confederacy. It was the lessons of the Civil War which led President Lincoln to back a project for a transcontinental railroad which was achieved by the famous meeting of the Union Pacific

Railroad and the Central Pacific Railroad at Promontory Point in 1869.

These lessons, like other military lessons of the Civil War, were largely ignored in Europe. Britain, not being a continental power, perhaps needed, less than others, to look to the strategic building of her internal rail routes, and clearly, fixed lines of track had their limitations in any war of rapid movement. They equally clearly had a supply role to play, but this was only slowly recognised. After ad hoc use of railways in Colonial wars, and following experience of the use of armoured trains in South Africa, British military planners saw a permanent role for railways in warfare. Thus, in 1906 they set up the Woolmer Instructional Military Railway (WIMR) near Liss in Hampshire. During World War I railway units trained at Woolmer played a very significant part in conveying the vast numbers of men and the great quantities of supplies needed to maintain the almost static front lines in Belgium and Northern France. Railway Transportation Officers, trained at the WIMR, also gave considerable assistance in the movement of men and equipment within Britain to the south coast ports for embarkation to Europe, and north to the great naval bases at Scapa Flow, Invergordon and Rosyth.

After the treaty of Versailles in 1919 and the final settlement of the Great War, like most other military units the facilities of the WIMR were run down. Obviously, in wartime military establishments must be larger than those required in peacetime, but the post-war reductions in Britain reached almost the point of extinction, and this was true of the WIMR. Fortunately, the establishment remained intact, and as war seemed increasingly possible in the 1930s, the facilities were expanded. In 1935 the establishment's name was changed to the 'Longmoor Military Railway'.

When war did begin the Longmoor facilities, ironically, were unable to meet all the demands of military railway training, so a second establishment was opened at Melbourne, near Derby, on a line taken over from the LMS Railway Company. In later chapters some of the work of Longmoor and Melbourne during World War II is reviewed, together with the associated Royal Engineers' Bridging School at King's Newton near Melbourne. We also look at some of the operations in theatres of war of units and individual people trained at the two establishments. Not only British engineers were trained; both Longmoor and Melbourne provided training and familiarisation courses for railway engineers from the Dominions and from the United States.

On 20th September, 1940 the *Derbyshire Advertiser* carried a feature on 'Railmen in Khaki' which concluded:

> This is a war of machines in which the engineer is perhaps even more important that the soldier, and speed in constructing and operating railways is likely to play its part in securing ultimate victory.

There can be no doubt that the truth of this comment was well proven by 1945, and we hope that later pages will show this. However, we also acknowledge that life in the wartime Services was not always grim, and we are glad to be able to relate some of the incidents which helped to lighten the burden of those years for these 'railmen in khaki'.

Chapter Two
'Ma, I Miss Your Apple Pie'
(The Longmoor Military Railway)

Begun in 1906 by the construction of a standard gauge line from Bordon station on the London and South Western Railway to Longmoor camp, the railway was known as the Woolmer Instructional Military Railway until 1935 when its name was changed to Longmoor Military Railway.

By 1922 little remained of the wartime establishment, but in the 1930s reconstruction began. In 1933 a line from Longmoor to Liss was completed together with the Hollywater loop. During World War II the Longmoor Military Railway had two important functions: to train tradesmen in transportation and to carry stores generated by Longmoor and Bordon camps. Passengers were carried by a service popularly known as 'The Bullet' which ran 19 times a day between Longmoor and Liss carrying eventually a daily total of 3,750 passengers. By 1944 some 22 locomotives were engaged in regular daily duties. The unit most closely associated with Longmoor was the 8th Railway Squadron. Formed originally in 1787 as the Guernsey and Jersey Company of the Royal Military Artificers, the Company served in the Peninsular War, at Waterloo and in the Crimean War. The Company became a Railway Company in 1882 and served in South Africa during the campaigns of 1899–1902, and was based at Longmoor from 1906. Throughout World War I the Company was on Line of Communication duties in France, and went to France in support of the BEF in 1939, a detachment serving in Palestine 1936–1940. The Company was sent to Norway in 1940 and was engaged on railway construction and operating duties in Northern Ireland 1940–1942. Following the invasion of Europe the Company was in North West Europe and Germany from 1944–1947.

10th Port Squadron also had a long association with Longmoor, but it did not have the continuous history of 8th Company. It was formed in 1805 as the Spike Island Company of the Royal Military Artificers, originally on detachment from the Woolwich Company, but was disbanded in 1819. It re-formed at Woolwich in 1839 and served in the so-called 'Kaffir Wars' of the 1840s and in the Crimea. Later the Squadron participated in the China Wars and in 1861–62 was commanded in Hong Kong by Capt. C.G. Gordon, later Major-General Gordon who ran out of steam at Khartoum. The Squadron was re-organised as a Railway Company in 1885 and was sent with Sir Garnet Wolseley's force to the Sudan in that year to attempt to rescue 'Chinese' Gordon. From 1899–1903 they were in South Africa and after a short spell at Woolwich were based at Longmoor 1905–1914 from where they joined 8th Company on Line of Communication duties in France. In 1920 the Company was disbanded, but reformed in 1924 only to be disbanded again on the very eve of war in 1939. In that year the Company reformed again in the Middle East from a detachment of 8th Company and a Railway Troop of 42nd Field Company. During the war the Company saw service in Eritrea, Palestine, Sicily, Austria and Italy and for a time was stationed with G.H.Q. Sudan at Khartoum in 1941.

The main purpose of Longmoor Military Railway was training of railway

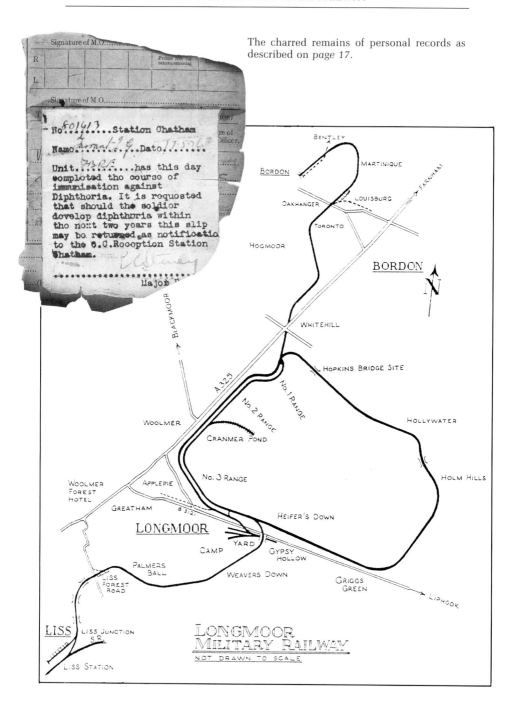

The charred remains of personal records as described on *page 17*.

operating troops. This included familiarising railway troops from overseas with European operating conditions. Large numbers of US transportation troops arrived for training in 1943–1944 and Canadian and Australian troops were also trained there.

The 8 mile line was single track except for about 1½ miles, and included along its length seven stations and a halt. With the Hollywater loop and marshalling yards, by 1939–40 the facilities were extensive but had not developed according to a grand design; they had grown and changed to meet new requirements. A regular daily timetable was operated to meet the transport requirements of a very large military area; as well as Royal Engineers, Royal Artillery units were based there and some infantry units. In 1940, for instance, a Company of the Sherwood Foresters was at Bordon camp. Civilians with business in the camp area were allowed to travel on this 'Longmoor Bullet', as it was nicknamed, without payment of fare but at their own risk.

The Centre was equipped to train men in all aspects of railway work, from surveying, through construction to operation, repair and maintenance. It was therefore to be expected that all types of railway craftsmen were found at Longmoor – engine drivers, firemen, signalmen, brakesmen, MT transport drivers and fitters, shunters, train controllers and clerks, while on the construction side were surveyors, draughtsmen, welders, plumbers, tin-smiths, carpenters and joiners. Men would work up through classifications 3, 2 and 1 according to the skills attained.

Signalling on the line was by various methods, mainly military flag signalling, but parts were controlled by semaphores and others by interlocked points. The Signalling School was well-equipped with lecture rooms and a demonstration room on the ground floor, and an electrically-operated model railway upstairs with a comprehensive track layout and sufficient stock to illustrate operating methods.

The stock of the line in 1939 consisted of six tank engines, mainly 0–6–0 and a large and varied collection of passenger, goods and mineral rolling stock. However, this stock was quickly supplemented on the outbreak of war mainly by requisition from British railway companies, and the locomotive stock was built up to 27 engines. When the 'Austerities' were introduced, Longmoor was their natural testing ground, and immediately prior to D-Day 300 such locomotives were in store awaiting transhipment to the Continent. Of these 200 were WD 2–8–0s and the rest WD 2–10–0s.

The operating loco stock in 1944 can be summarised as follows:

- 2– 2–10–0 tender engines ⎫ North British
- 3– 2–8–0 tender engines ⎬
- 12– 0–6–0 saddle tanks mainly by Hunslet, but one each from Robert Stephenson and Hawthorn, and the Vulcan foundry
- 1– 0–6–0 side tank
- 4– Diesels
- 5– Diesel Electric from various makers but, one, interestingly, a development of the LMS and English Electric.

The engines were not always treated with the respect they deserved. The story is told of a locomotive which found its way along the line to the ashpits

A U.S.A. 0–6–0 tank locomotive re-painted, numbered and named *Frank S. Ross* seen here at the Longmoor Military Railway. *Authors' Collection*

A typical activity at Longmoor! The re-railing of the tank locomotive *Earl Roberts*. 'Easy when you know how.' *Authors' Collection*

without benefit of driver. Locomotives required for the day's work had been lit up and were building up steam pressure in the shed when QMS (I) Green, the Warrant Officer in charge of the shed, heard a loud bang and saw an engine getting under way. 'Who the . . . is moving that loco?' he shouted. The only reply was the rending of the shuttered doors at the shed end as the engine burst through and made off down the line, adorned with the shed door. At the first signal the door caught the signal stanchion and fell far enough to be caught between the bogies and the rail. As it was thus drawn off the engine, the latter ran over the steel door with a terrific noise. The points were set for the ash tip and the locomotive, now free of its encumbrance and on a falling gradient, ran merrily on until it crashed into the buffers, demolishing them and toppling over the end of the embankment into marshy ground where it lay issuing forth steam from every seam.

CSM Tarrant who tells the story goes on to say that the subsequent Court of Inquiry found that the hand brake had not been applied, the regulator was partially open and when it had been parked the position of the pistons was just right to set the locomotive in motion when the head of steam built up sufficiently. The loud 'bang' which alerted 'Dodger' Green to the moving engine was the clearance of condensed water in the jackets, there being no blow-cocks open.

In 1942 a Transportation Stores Depot opened with a complement of 154 men and 1,500 tons of stores. By 1944 the personnel numbered 1,500 and the stores area covered 150 acres, handling 50,000 tons per month.

In 1939 approximately 4,000 trained military railwaymen were available. By the end of the war 146,000 were engaged in military railway work and most of these passed through Longmoor at least once. One Company Commander was quoted in the *Railway Magazine* of November–December 1946: 'You can tell a Longmoor-trained Sapper anywhere, but you can't tell him much.'

Longmoor's role in initial training was not that envisaged for it during the 1930s. A scheme was developed for each of the four great railway companies to provide and maintain a military railway unit. This Supplementary Reserve would provide units of men who would need to be called up for a week or so every other year for military training (but not for technical training). A good idea if it had worked, but it did not. When war came it was found that many Reservists were not of the trade for which they were declared. For example a 'Blacksmith Class I' turned out to be a District Engineer's Saloon Attendant! Other Reservists were medically unfit for regular military service, and many others did not arrive at their units at Longmoor because they were needed to train other railway staff for war work.

So from the outset of the war trainees were received direct from the Labour Exchanges. Every fortnight 250 men arrived to receive three months' training; two weeks' general recruit work, medicals and kitting out; eight weeks' technical training; two weeks 'on the square' and preparation for posting. It was not the best preparation for the job to be done, 'but somewhere, somehow each square peg would be adapted to fill a useful hole.' British railway operating troops were based in Iran and Iraq, India, Burma, the Middle East, West Africa and Ceylon. When troops were later required for service in Italy and France, they were in almost all cases drawn from units who had seen service elsewhere and were very rarely fresh ex-depot.

Traffic built up to a peak in September 1944 and when Mr A.R. Gillitt arrived at Longmoor early in 1944 as assistant locomotive superintendent some 70 miles of track were operation. His subsequent experience shows the value of Longmoor training. In December 1944 he joined (for the second time) No. 182 Railway Operating Company in Eindhoven, Holland. A detachment was sent to Nijmegen after its liberation, and built up from nothing a railway organisation handling 40,000 tons of stores per week just before the Rhine crossing in March 1945.

However, such superb organisation was not the impression gained by many on arrival at Longmoor! Mr Bernard Cloake has given us his first impressions of Longmoor when he arrived to join the MT section. 'I wasn't too happy for it seemed all so isolated, and for miles around nothing but troops and camps, and all I seemed to do was guard duties, parades, drill and quite often menial duties, which of course I resented. Discipline was extremely strict and for me it was all rather uninteresting.' Not surprising, since Mr Cloake had just spent four months on a fitter's course at the Northampton Polytechnic College at Islington in the excitement (for a young survivor) of the blitz on London.

In the early days of the war the Motor Transport Section at Longmoor boasted only two vehicles – a Morris 15 cwt. lorry and a 15 cwt. Guy. The total MT personnel numbered nine, but by 1941 there were 60 personnel and a considerable increase in the number of vehicles. There were about 50 vehicles of all types with evocative names like BSA, Ariel and Hillman. Every vehicle was carefully maintained. Drivers were responsible for greasing and general maintenance but each month the vehicles had a routine check by fitters, faults being rectified or new parts fitted. Every detail was entered in 'the 406' or vehicle log book. The next step was a road test by Sgt Fox and the fitter who had carried out the work. This welcome break from camp environs and routine was always completed by a visit to a cafe at Liphook, and egg and chips whenever rations permitted.

The duties of the MT section were many and various, but required personnel to be on duty at all hours. The following account may give an idea of the variety of duties.

Rations had to be collected from Aldershot and distributed to Longmoor, Martinique, Apple Pie, Weaver's Down, Woolmer, Bordon. Bread was collected from Bordon and one driver had a lucrative private delivery service operating alongside this 'bread run'. One of our correspondents claims that 'soldiering and fiddling were a combined operation throughout the Services' and that someone could always find a way round any rule or regulation.

Another duty was to pick up new vehicles from depots in the south of England and this could involve two or three days away from camp. There was always a roadside café to be found where soldiers were well treated despite rationing; most people had a close relative in one of the Services and this provided a bond among people who were strangers to each other.

When required, drivers would take men of the Special Squadron Raiding Parties (known inevitably as the SS) a few miles from the camp. They then had to carry out training tasks and return to camp on foot. Other duties included collection of clothing from Aldershot for distribution to all parts of the Longmoor camps, provision of coal from the camp coal yard to all cookhouse and barrack blocks, and to provide officers' transport as and when required. As Mr George Grouch puts it: 'One was at beck and call for anything that was to move or to pick up'. The usual duty squad after the arrival of the ATS was two male drivers, two ATS drivers and one duty corporal, late turn for the men being 5 pm until Reveille the next morning and for the ATS 5 pm to 10 pm.

The need for drivers to be always available was obvious and for that reason the MT section was excused all parades except the pay parade, although even that was staggered. There was one occasion when a senior officer ordered that MT section would parade with all Other Ranks at 07.30 hrs. Of course the order was obeyed with resulting chaos all over the camp. By 10.30 'phone lines were hot with cookhouses, Sergeants' Mess, Officers' Mess and ATS Mess all complaining of non-delivery of rations. Hitler's heart would have been gladdened had he known that in deepest Hampshire the British Army was on the verge of mutiny as it was discovered that there was no milk for the tea! So ended the one and only full parade of the MT Section.

Army cooking is well remembered. Cookhouses at Longmoor were in the main clean, modern and spacious, but catering for the great numbers involved meant that results could be charitably described as 'mediocre' although there was always a good Sunday roast. There was also a NAAFI and a Church of England Institute for evening snacks. Bernard Cloake says, 'I preferred the C. of E. for you could get Horlicks which to me was nectar after NAAFI tea!

Entertainment was provided by ENSA, and the MT Section was called upon to transport entertainment stars of the day. Naturally much of the entertainment was of the home grown variety as will be seen. Here mention should be made of the 'Flying Bull' at Rake, centre for much riotous entertainment. With wartime lighting restrictions, driving back to camp could be an adventure in itself, although there seem to have been no accidents of consequence or even any serious brushes with either civilian or military police: perhaps it is that none of our correspondents actually remembers any details of those drives back to camp.

Ken Smethurst worked as a shunter/guard for the LMS in Yorkshire but volunteered for military service on the outbreak of war. His initial wish was to join the RAF with his pal, but he found that as a railwayman, if he went into the RE Railway Section his money would be made up and sent to his mother. With Army pay at 2s. per day (10p) this was an important consideration so Ken joined the Royal Engineers. His pal Alec was later killed flying over Germany.

Ken went first to Longmoor for six weeks' military training but after three weeks was posted to Derby and the Melbourne Military Railway, much to his pleasure for he had not found Longmoor to his liking. Stationed at

Bordon camp, he found it 'very regimental' and they were on fatigues within days of arrival. The whole point of the period at Longmoor of course was to instil military discipline, but it left scope for individual initiative. One of Ken's jobs was to take coke round to the Sergeants' Messes and other places. His company were allocated camp beds to sleep on and 'it was absolutely cold . . . it was deadly. We spent the first night frozen . . . I never slept at all'. There was only one light bulb in the billet too.

Both problems were soon remedied. One light bulb from each Mess visited fixed up the lighting in the billet and a bathful of coke from the back of the NAAFI provided some warmth. The bathful of coke was carried right through Bordon Camp without challenge. Another example of bold initiative yielding best results.

Longmoor, however, did find itself as it were 'in the front line' on two occasions. On 13th August, 1940 the 8th Military Training Battalion R.E. was at Apple Pie Camp when the first bombing attack occurred. The raid took place at about 06.30 and was carried out by Luftwaffe aircraft apparently unable to penetrate the London defences and looking for targets of opportunity as they made their way back to their base. As well as bombing, the aircraft strafed the area with machine gun fire; no air-raid warning was given and three men were killed. Mr G.R.T. Evans who enlisted in the 8th Training Battalion in November 1939 tells of his experience of the attack:

> The first indication we had of the raid was a whistling sound followed by a loud explosion and then obvious panic. Not many knew the location of the slit trenches so one can well understand the fearful situation. As far as I know there was only one Bren gun post at the camp – not really of much defence against an attack of that magnitude.

A number of delayed-action bombs were discovered and dealt with by RE Bomb Disposal Squads, but the raid left all personnel at Apple Pie Camp shaken and nervous.

The *Railway Magazine* of November–December 1946 had this interesting comment on the incident:

> In the summer of 1940 Apple Pie Camp was distinguished for the geometrical neatness of its rows of tents; lines of kit were dressed in front and each kit was surmounted by a gleaming mess-tin. The first flight of Junkers to arrive eyed this inviting display with some suspicion before accepting the too-good-to-be-true evidence at face value.

The BBC announced that bombs had been dropped on waste ground in Hampshire. It seemed, two days later, that the Luftwaffe had not believed this tale for air raid sirens alerted the inhabitants of Longmoor again. This time the men were evacuated in orderly fashion and found shelter in deep trenches in a wood as the enemy aircraft approached. The raid was directed at Longmoor camp itself, and though a pillar of smoke hung over Longmoor, there were no casualties.

Some time later the men were alerted again. Each man at Apple Pie Camp was given a rifle and ammunition and all were kept on general alert for two or three days. This was at the height of the Nazi invasion scare, and the warning of imminent danger from elite Wehrmacht parachutists was given by a trumpeter riding round the camps on the back of a lorry.

Even bombing could have its amusing aspects, usually in retrospect. CSM I.G. Tarrant recalls an officer being very annoyed at the Luftwaffe's uninvited attentions to his car. He had parked it near to the MT Office and a piece of shrapnel had sliced through the rim of his spare wheel, ruining both wheel and tyre. The metal had continued through the back of the car ripping along the rear seat and finally coming to rest in the dashboard.

CSM Tarrant managed to save a small personal memento of the incendiary attack on the MT Office. The charred remains of his own records in the files are reproduced on page 10.

After the invasion scare had passed, RE drivers at Longmoor began to be replaced by ATS. The fitters were retained together with a number of male drivers of lower medical grades. ATS personnel had actually been stationed at Longmoor since the outbreak of the war. The first unit to arrive was the 11th County of London Company, formed at Hammersmith in November 1939 and attached to Princess Louise's Kensington Regiment. They arrived at Longmoor on 28th September, 1939, travelling from Liss to Longmoor in coaches of 1914–18 vintage marked '40 Hommes, 18 Chevaux'.

The arrival of female personnel was not entirely welcomed by REs, although some were clearly ready to make the most of the opportunity. REs and RAs packed the entrance to the quarters as the girls arrived at dusk. Suddenly, above the general hubbub, a male voice was heard 'I've got mine!', to be answered swiftly by a female voice; 'Let me go at once, I'm the Company Commander!' The first priority thereafter was to make the approaches to the ATS quarters out of bounds to the RE. This was seen only as a spur to ingenuity and many romances blossomed, not a few into marriage.

Volunteer Pimm remembers her arrival at Longmoor as a bit of a muddle. Although many had enlisted as storewomen, they became cooks or orderlies. The standard of cooking was not high – one volunteer took 24 hours to cook a cabbage! The duties undertaken by the ATS became more diverse as the war went on. Pte Ruby Relf arrived at Longmoor in January 1940 and worked as cashier at the Camp Cinema, later organising a team of cashiers, and eventually became CSM after transferring to ATS Administration.

Volunteer Pimm remembers the bombing attack on Apple Pie Camp very well. Shortly after inspecting the bomb damage she and a colleague saw unexploded bombs go off close to where they had been standing.

Longmoor was used as a reception centre for returning REs and such of their equipment as had been salvaged from Dunkirk. ATS personnel spent hours making sandwiches, and both then and when the camp was attacked, Red Cross-trained ATS personnel were required to sleep at the Reception Station and never leave the camp. Much as this was necessary work, it was tiring and frustrating; an order to attend fire drills was ignored, and when on fatigues the Volunteers organised a 'Dig for Victory' effort. These 'nose thumbings' at authority did not go unnoticed; the CO was replaced rather smartly.

For some at least of 11th County of London Company ATS the war almost came much closer. In May 1940 Volunteers Seeley and Pimm were posted to join the British Expeditionary Force in France. They had not only had all their vaccinations and their embarkation leave, but had been given a 'lovely farewell party' when all was cancelled. What a disappointment, but perhaps just as well as the BEF was at that moment fighting its way to Dunkirk. In March 1941 the 11th County of London Company was disbanded, but ATS personnel continued to serve at Longmoor for the duration of the war.

Of course, Longmoor was concerned chiefly with the training of railway staffs of all kinds. Driver Jim Roberts was perhaps typical of many who trained for their military service on the Longmoor Military Railway. After driving Peckett locomotives on public works for McAlpine's he joined the Royal Engineers in June 1940 and went to Longmoor for basic military training where he came under the guiding hand and voice of RSM Dimmock, remembered by many who had only a brief stay there as 'Mr Longmoor'. From Longmoor Jim Roberts went to Bedford for familiarisation on all types of engines and routes and then to Gourock, working dockside railways loading vessels in support of troops going overseas.

For three years, however, Jim Roberts was driving locomotives hauling ammunition trains at Marlborough Farm, near Kineton. Locomotives in use at Kineton were from varied sources, mainly private builders like Hunslet, Hawthorn Leslie and Beyer-Garretts, but there were also a number of ex-French locomotives. The men, incidentally, were housed in a number of ex-French railway carriages, eight men to each carriage.

The sub-structure of the lines was poor and it was not uncommon for locomotives and their ammunition trains to leave the tracks. Although fairly common, such incidents always required the submission of a full report and not all enginemen were trained in this particular art. One driver was admonished for presenting reports which were too long. Shortly afterwards he crashed a train into the doors which protected the entrance to the ammunition dump and presented his report thus:

> The wind blew,
> The door went to,
> And I went through.

The very soul of clarity and brevity!

Military drivers usually wore blue dungarees and peaked caps and looked like civilian train crews. It was not difficult therefore for military train crews to travel on civilian trains as if they were replacement crews – no tickets were needed for men who had, for example, 'just taken a train to Scotland'. They had little need to turn out on parade either. The one major parade at Kineton received a somewhat back-handed compliment from the inspecting general. As the parade came to the 'General Salute' he remarked that the bayonet-fitted rifles glinted beautifully 'like a field of waving corn'.

RE personnel naturally worked very hard at the tasks for which they had trained. One fitter at Kineton volunteered for regular night duties, a turn time from 22.00 to 06.00. At 07.30 a Northampton–Stratford train stopped to pick up passengers at Marlborough Farm. Soldiers were allowed to take on casual labour and the RE mechanic worked as a fitter in the Stratford engine sheds. He did this for 3½ years working as a civilian loco-fitter by day and as a military loco-fitter by night. When did he sleep? His military tasks were concerned with minor repairs to locomotives worked by crews on the 08.00–17.00 shift and drivers would record jobs required in a repairs book. Some repairs were accompanied by an unobtrusive code of dots indicating that the work was not actually required. The job was then booked as completed and it was possible for the fitter to sleep for at least a part of the night.

Jim Roberts also undertook casual labour, working on a nearby farm, especially at harvest time. He developed a particular skill in building stocks of corn sheaves, not a skill in-bred to those born in Liverpool. As in so many cases, the friendship formed between Jim and his farming friends during the war has continued to this day.

Eventually Jim Roberts left Kineton for Faslane where he worked trains building up supplies for the invasion of Europe and where invasion practice was taking place continuously.

This account is typical of the wartime experience of many REs – a dangerous task carried out over a long period and making a vital contribution to the national effort to pursue the war successfully.

Railway Traffic Officers were also trained at Longmoor for service on railways both within Britain and abroad. Such officers had played an important role in easing the movement of personnel in liaison with the staffs of the civilian Railway Companies during World War I and their value was recognised in the formation of a Movement Control Group in 1938. This was part of the Supplementary Reserve, and the Group received the standard two weeks' training at Longmoor in 1938 and the summer of 1939. By September 1939 two more Groups had been formed but had not received military training when they went to France in support of the BEF; two more Groups followed quite soon.

From September 1939 to June 1941 the training of Movement Control personnel switched to the Melbourne Military Railway, but then, after a short spell at Aberford near Leeds, the training base was again switched back to Longmoor in September 1941. There the work of Movement Control personnel was developed and extended. Their role now became much more complex than that of their counterparts in 1914–18. It was recognised that Movement Control officers would need to work as part of a combined operations team in assisting opposed beach landings, and even at home the work of the RTOs would be complicated as rail journeys were likely to be interrupted by enemy aircraft. In 1940, for instance, Lord Stamp, Chairman of the LMS, received a letter of complaint from a journalist whose scheduled journey of two hours took more than eight hours. He complained that in one spell of two hours the train moved forward only by 1½ miles although he acknowledged that the total distance covered had been greater than that as the train had been travelling backwards for some of the time! The reason for all this was quite simply that the Luftwaffe were giving the lines ahead their destructive attention. Civilian railway staff and RTOs were fully occupied in keeping the train on lines heading roughly in the right direction, and certainly LMS officials regarded such criticisms as very unfair on their hard-pressed staff.

After Dunkirk, Movement Control units were concerned with the re-organisation of BEF units and their re-deployment for home defence, Long-moor itself being a concentrating ground for much of the equipment salvaged by all kinds of units in their retreat from France. Following this period they were occupied with the embarkation of troops for North Africa and the Middle East, and dealing with the effects of air attack on the railways and ports handling this traffic.

The Official History records that the construction of military ports at Faslane and Cairn Ryan gave opportunities for training in Movement Control not available at civilian ports, and that the most significant contribution of Movement Control to the war effort was in assisting the concentration of 21st Army Group near the south coast before D-Day.

However, Movement Control did have its lapses and one such came with the despatch of a force to Iceland in 1940. The Official History tells how the newly-trained RTOs left the boats eager to go about their duties only to discover that Iceland had no railways!

Some details of the work of Longmoor men overseas are given in later chapters but the records of two Companies are given here to indicate the variety of experience which befell these military railmen.

153 Railway Operating Company

1.5.40	L. of C.*	France BEF
20.4.42	L. of C.	Persia
19.8.42		10th Army
29.5.43	GHQ	Palestine
15.3.44		Italy
26.9.44		Sicily

190 Railway Operating Company

1.6.40	South of R. Somme (France)
20.4.42	Persia Base L. of C.
29.5.43	GHQ Palestine
7.7.43	GHQ 15th Army Group (Sicily)
15.8.43	Italy
26.9.44	8th Army
9.12.44	Sicily

* Lines of Communication

A Dean Goods locomotive (without numberplate) on loan from the Great Western Railway to the Longmoor Military Railway. Note the Longmoor Military Railway brake van.   *Authors' Collection*

Chapter Three
'Slow Freight'
(The Melbourne Military Railway)

Unlike the Longmoor Military Railway, the facilities at Melbourne in South Derbyshire were requisitioned from a civil railway company for the duration of the war only. Thus the Melbourne Military Railway has a longer chronological history than Longmoor while having only a comparatively brief existence as a military training establishment.

The Midland Railway opened its branch line to Ashby-de-la-Zouch in Leicestershire progressively between 1868 and 1874. The purpose of the line was to connect the market-gardening district around Melbourne with Derby, the chief market town of the area. It also improved transport facilities for the Cloud Hill Lime Works at Breedon-on-Cloud-Hill, and later for small collieries between Melbourne and Ashby.

Plans for this railway were deposited at Derby on 30th November, 1863:

> A Railway to commence in the parish of Normanton in the County of Derby, by a junction with the Midland Railway at a point twenty-one chains, or said thereabouts north eastward of the place where the said Midland Railway passes under the public highway, leading from Derby and Normanton to Sinfin Moor, and to terminate in the parish of Breedon-on-the-Hill in the County of Leicester, by a junction with a certain Railway and Tramway belonging to the Company leading from Cloud Hill Lime Works to Ashby-de-la-Zouch.

In May 1864 Parliamentary approval was granted for the Midland Railway to build the Normanton and Breedon line, 9 miles 9½ chains from a junction with the Derby to Bristol main line at Normanton to an end-on connection with the Ashby and Cloud Hill Tramway at Breedon, together with a junction branch 48½ chains long at Normanton, but this latter curve of a proposed triangular junction at Normanton was never constructed.

On 30th November, 1864 the Midland deposited another set of plans for further 'New Lines and Additional Powers':

> A Railway to commence in the parish of Breedon-on-the-Hill in the County of Leicester, by a junction with the Railway first described (The Normanton and Breedon) and authorised by the Midland Railway (New Lines and Additional Powers) Act 1864 at the termination thereof in the said parish of Breedon-on-the-Hill and to terminate in the parish of Ashby in the County of Leicester, by a junction with the Leicester and Burton Line of the Midland Railway, at a point three hundred and forty yards or thereabouts westward of the Ashby-de-la-Zouch Station of the Railway.

A further Act dated 5th July, 1865 authorised the conversion of the 4ft 2in. gauge Ashby and Cloud Hill Tramway into a standard gauge railway.

The Normanton to Breedon stretch was a new line, but the Ashby and Breedon would be the conversion of an existing tramway. This 4ft 2in. gauge tramway linked the Cloud Hill Lime Works with the Ashby Canal at Willersley basin, and was authorised – together with Ticknall Tramway – on 1st April, 1799. It came into use between July and October 1802, and in order to discourage competition in the Leicestershire coalfield – the Great

21

A view of Chellaston and Swarkestone station in Midland days as seen on an old postcard.
Lens of Sutton

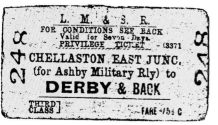

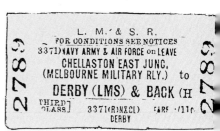

Chellaston Quarry sidings photographed in 1954 with the signal box still in LMS Livery.
G.A. Yeomans

A view of the entry line to King's Newton Depot in April 1954. *G.A. Yeomans*

A Ministry of Supply locomotive seen here at King's Newton exchange sidings in April 1958. The engine crew deliberately turned their backs on the photographer so as not to be identified. *G.A. Yeomans*

An early view of Melbourne station in 1907 with an up passenger train pulling into the station.   G.A. Yeomans Collection

An LMS class '2P', No. 495 on a down train to Derby seen here on the last day of passenger service on the line, September 1930.   G.A. Yeomans Collection

A Sunday afternoon engineer's train at Melbourne in 1950 with a LMS class '3F' 0–6–0 in charge.
G.A. Yeomans

Good Friday 1958 with No. 44232 ready to leave Melbourne with a freight train.
G.A. Yeomans

Again Good Friday 1958 with No. 41 trip working from New Lount crossing No. 44232 waiting for the road.
G.A. Yeomans

The single line station of Tonge and Breedon seen here in April 1954. Note the ground frame hut. *G.A. Yeomans*

MIDLAND RAILW.
Issued subject to the R... ...ions & Conditions
stated in the Company's ...e Tables & Bills.
THIRD CLASS. THIRD CLASS.
AVAILABLE ON DAY OF ISSUE ONLY.
DERBY to
TONGE & BREEDON
Fare 8½d.
Derby-T & Breedon
Fare 8½d.
Derby-T & Breedon

A livestock special seen on 31st March, 1960 at Tonge and Breedon station. This train was a farm removal for Mr Dibb-Smith of Breedon Brand to St Erth in Cornwall.
G.A. Yeomans Collection

A very early photograph at Worthington showing the entrance to the Breedon & Cloud Hill Lime Co's sidings in Midland Railway days.   *G.A. Yeomans Collection*

Clearing up after the accident on 14th June, 1955 at the Breedon & Cloud Hill Lime Co. sidings near Worthington. The station can be seen at the top of the photograph.   *G.A. Yeomans Collection*

A view of the entry to the sidings for the Leicestershire Colliery & Pipe Co. Note the loading wharf now derelict (April 1957).   *G.A. Yeomans*

0–4–0ST, *George Stephenson* built 1924 by Hawthorn Leslie Co. Note the lower oval plate which carries the words, 'The Leicestershire Colliery & Pipe Co. Ltd, Lount'. Seen here in September 1955.   *Frank Jones*

The entry to New Lount Colliery sidings and adjacent ground frame, seen here in April 1957.

G.A. Yeomans

MIDLAND RAILWAY. This Ticket is issued subject to the Regulations & Conditions stated in the Company's Time Tables & Bills.

THIRD CLASS.   THIRD CLASS.
AVAILABLE ON DAY OF ISSUE ONLY.

(A) Manchester (Vic.) to
WORTHINGTON
Via Ancoats Junc. & Marple
FARE 5s. 8½d.   FARE 5s. 8½d.
A)M'chester \ Worthington A)M'chester \ Worthington

Worthington station as seen in April 1954 with the quarry in the background.

G.A. Yeomans

Ticknall sidings (sometimes called Ticknall Wharf).

R.C. Riley Collection

Burton Road Crossing ground frame seen here in April 1957.

G.A. Yeomans

Ashby station with the main line signal box visible in the distance.

Lens of Sutton

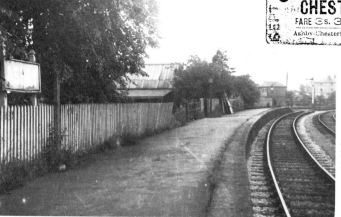

Northern Railway and the London and North Western Railway – the Midland, by virtue of an Act dated 16th July, 1864, bought up the Ashby Canal Company and its associated tramways for £110,000. These tramways were worked by horses, the Cloud Hill to Ashby section remaining so until conversion to standard gauge railway.

For pressing financial reasons the Midland Railway Company opened the line in three short stages:

Melbourne Junction to Melbourne ....1st September, 1868 – double track
Melbourne to Worthington ....1st October, 1869 – single track
Worthington to Ashby-de-la-Zouch ....1st January, 1874 – single track

The map on page 6 shows the line of the branch railway from its junction with the West of England main line at Melbourne Junction, to Ashby. Six stations were provided on the line as follows:

Chellaston (re-named Chellaston and Swarkestone in 1901). This station was situated 3 miles 71 chains from Derby London Road Junction and was provided with two platforms. A station master's office and a booking hall were built on the up platform, and a waiting shelter on the down platform. The buildings were constructed of timber, and platform lighting was by gas. A station signal box and a two-road goods yard were situated immediately south of the station on the up side, a goods shed being constructed astride the siding. A one-ton crane was installed in the 1930s, but removed shortly after nationalisation of the railways. There were also facilities for loading and unloading livestock, but these were withdrawn in 1961.

Melbourne. The station here marked the end of the double track section of the line, and was approached through a short cutting and under a small road bridge. There were two platforms, the down side being provided with a single-storey timber building comprising station master's office, booking office and waiting room, while the up side boasted a single waiting shelter, also of timber construction. Melbourne Station signal box stood at the south end of the down platform, and beyond the cattle pens, and controlled access to the three-road goods yard. Part of the siding was covered by a large timber-built goods shed which contained a 1 t. 10 cwt. crane, but these were removed in 1955. The station was actually three-quarters of a mile from the centre of Melbourne, and was much more convenient for the inhabitants of King's Newton only a quarter of a mile away.

Wilson. This small, single-platform station was opened for passenger and parcel traffic only, but its life lasted barely two years from 1st October, 1869 until 1st June, 1871.

Tonge and Breedon. Another single-platform station with a single-storey brick-built station building on the down side. Until 1948 an old Midland Railway Pullman Car body stood at the Wilson end of the platform, but it was broken up. During occupation by the Melbourne Military Railway the goods yard was enlarged to accommodate a passing loop, and two sidings were laid alongside the boundary fence. These provided end-loading facilities parallel to the loop-siding and together they were designated War Department Siding (Castle Donington) and could be utilised for loading or off-loading Army vehicles in connection with the Motor Vehicle MU at

Donington Park. In LMS days an auxiliary tablet instrument was installed at Tonge and Breedon, and another one in Melbourne box thus enabling a train to be held inside the long loop siding while the Melbourne–Worthington tablet was released for a through train.

Worthington. This had a single platform on the down side on which was erected a waiting shelter of wooden construction. Just beyond the station and parallel to the running line was Shields' Siding from which extended a long shunting siding that ran alongside the station approach road. Worthington signal box stood on the opposite side of the line to the platform, as did a single-storey building erected during the last war. It was from Worthington that the real climb began, the gradient steepening from 1 in 104 to 1 in 60, and a number of sidings led off at different points to serve various works and collieries along the line. The most important of these were the Lount Colliery sidings which served New Lount Colliery, opened in 1925. There were also Cloud Hill Lime Works sidings as well as sidings to the pipe works which, since their inception in 1898, had traded under various names, the last of which was settled in 1956 as the Newbold Pipe Works.

After passing through the 308 yds-long Ashby Tunnel the line passed over Smisby Road, then, via level crossings, it crossed the Burton Road, High Street and Tamworth Road to reach Ashby station. From there it joined the Leicester and Burton line at Ashby Junction. The existence of the three aforementioned level crossings caused the military engineers to close *their* line at Smisby Road.

The original intention of the Midland Railway was to run the line mainly as a freight line, so passenger services were, therefore, infrequent. The first section of the line began operating without any official opening ceremony on 1st September, 1868, and on the following day an official notice appeared in the *Derby Mercury* which stated:

MIDLAND RAILWAY
OPENING OF THE MELBOURNE BRANCH

On Tuesday, September 1st the Railway between DERBY and MELBOURNE will be opened for Passenger and Goods Traffic and until further notice Trains will run as under:

DERBY TO MELBOURNE

		am	pm	pm
Derby	dep.	8.50	1.45	6.45
Chellaston	arr.	9.04	1.59	6.59
Melbourne	arr.	9.15	2.10	7.10

MELBOURNE TO DERBY

Melbourne	dep.	9.40	2.35	7.35
Chellaston	arr.	9.50	2.45	7.45
Derby	arr.	10.05	3.00	8.00

JAMES ALLPORT
General Manager

Derby, August 1868

By February, 1869 there were four trains each way, the additional train being the 4.00 pm from Derby, returning from Melbourne at 4.45 pm. The service was extended to Worthington on 1st October the same year, and

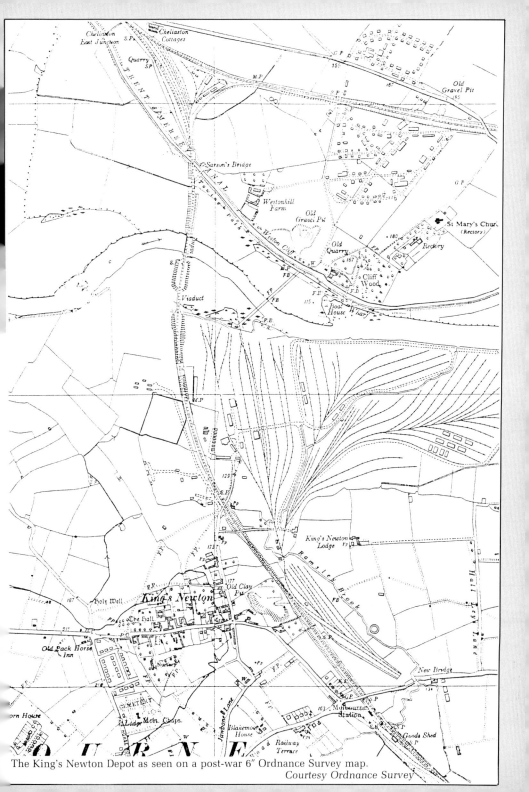

The King's Newton Depot as seen on a post-war 6″ Ordnance Survey map.
Courtesy Ordnance Survey

Worthington remained as passenger terminus until 1st January, 1874 when a passenger service was brought into operation between Derby and Ashby. A typical timetable of this later period is that of 1878: departures from Derby were at 10.40 am, 2.05, and 7.00 pm, with a 4.20 pm on Fridays only to Worthington. Departures from Ashby in the reverse direction were at 8.30, 11.40 am, and 4.15 pm. During the months of May to October an additional short working to Melbourne was introduced departing Derby at 5.40 pm, and returning from Melbourne at 7.30 pm, but this train did not run on Fridays. It is noticeable, perhaps, that there was no Sunday service.

This omission was rectified and by May 1886 additional workings had been brought into operation including a Sunday service to Worthington from Derby at 5.00 pm. However, although this was booked as a passenger service, time was allowed on the return journey for loading milk at Tonge and Breedon as well as at Melbourne, and the train left Worthington at 5.35 pm, and returned to Trent.

An interesting development in passenger traffic was the introduction of a steam railmotor service on 1st March, 1906. This followed on from trials which had been run on the Wirksworth branch and the Ripley branch as well as the Melbourne branch. It was a 3rd class, weekdays only operation, and the railmotor left Derby at 7.40 am, 12.05, and 4.45 pm, the last being a Fridays Excepted working. By October 1906 the service had been reduced to two railmotors a day, but locomotive-hauled trains continued until, by April 1910, the daily service comprised five loco-hauled trains and two steam railmotor workings.

In July 1921 the passenger service was established in a more-or-less set pattern which would last until all passenger services were withdrawn on 22nd September, 1930. Departures from Derby were: 8.25, 10.20 am, 1.10, 2.44, 5.53, and 7.33 pm, with a late-night Saturdays Only train to Melbourne at 10.45 pm. This last train returned to Derby as empty stock. In the reverse direction a train left Melbourne at 7.00 am, its coaching stock having come out from Derby at 6.15 am. Thereafter departures from Ashby were at 8.03, 9.37, and 11.15 am. There was a 1.55 pm from Melbourne that actually started from Worthington at 1.45, on Saturdays, then followed the 3.55 pm and 7.15 pm, from Ashby.

On 1st January, 1923, as a result of the Railways Act of 1921, the Derby to Ashby line became part of the Midland Division of the newly-formed London, Midland and Scottish Railway, and although a 5.12 pm (SX) Derby to Melbourne was introduced in 1924 – returning at 6.02 pm – it became apparent that modifications to the timetable were imminent. In September 1927 the 8.25 am Derby to Ashby and the 9.37 am Ashby to Derby were suspended, and the 1.10 pm Derby to Worthington became a Saturdays Only train. The 10.45 pm (SO) Derby to Melbourne was also taken off.

Without doubt it was the bus service introduced by the Trent Motor Traction Company in the 1920s that succeeded in reducing the railway's passenger traffic between Derby, Melbourne and Ashby, and on 22nd September, 1930 the line became a freight only facility. The agricultural products for which the line had, in the first place, been opened continued to

WEEKDAYS.   **SUNDAYS**

DERBY — dep.	7 28	12	8 30	9 5		9 30	10 32	11 50		10	12 5	2 22	3 15	5 7		5 38	5 52	6 52	7 45	7 52	8 15		10 40		5 0	
Pear Tree & Normanton	7 34	8		9 8			10 35	11 54		14		2 28				5 47		6 57		7 55	8 1	8 24			7 52	5 1	8 6
Chellast'n & Swarkest'ne		8 39	9 14				10 41	12 2		20		2 35				5 52	6 1							
Melbourne		8 44					10 48				2 45				4 59		6 9		8 7					5 15	
Tonge & Breedon		8 50					10 54				2 52				5 6		6 14		8 13					5 22	
Worthington		8 55					10 59				2 59				5 16		6 24		8 18					5 24	
ASHBY — arr.		9 5					11 10				3 15				5 27		6 31		8 29					5 27	
Birmingham dep.			8 52			12 10								4 32					5 0						
Burton "			9 52			12 55								5 18					5 34						
Ashby "	8 22				11 20								4 10			7 10		7 10							
Weston-on-Trent	30				12 9		7 26						5 55			8 1		8 32				7 58		6 11	
Castle Donington																									
& Shardlow	8 8	42	7 20	9 35	10 17	10 22	12 16		7 34	1 59	4 12	5 35	5 45	6 2	7 29	8	8 39	10 27	5 18	6 21	
TRENT { arr.	7 30	9 35			12 25	1 22	45				5 55	6 10			8 15	8 49	9 30	11 30	8 18	6 33	
{ dep.	7 35	9 48			12 34	1 49	0		2	6				8 23	5 40	9 36	12 20	8 33	7 20	
Attenboro' arr.							2			6 19			8 27	8 33				
Beeston "	7 42	54			45	8			6 24							1 26	
Nottingham "	7 50	10 3	10 36		12 44	1 54	10		6 12	6 32		8 30	0 10	0 50	1 35	8 45	7 35	

WEEKDAYS.   **SUNDAYS**

Nottingham dep.	6 32		7 35	8 20		10 0		1 15	3 3		3 50	5 12		7 0		10 40		
Beeston	6 40		7 42	8 27				1 24	3 10		3 57			7 7		10 47		
Attenboro'									3 14								
TRENT { arr.	6 46		7 48	8 33		10 10		1 30	3 19		4 3	5 22		7 10		10 53		
{ dep.	7 0		7 55	8 35		10 13		1 50	3 30		4 5	5 25		7 18		11 10		
Castle Donington																		
& Shardlow	7 10	7 20	8 5	8 42		9 26	10 22	12 16	7 34	1 59		4 12	5 35	6 2	7 29	8	8 7 18	11 11	8 7	6 21
Weston-on-Trent			8 14			10 28			2 5				7 39			
Ashby arr.			9 5			11 10			3 15				8 29			
Burton "			9 1						3 55		4 31					
Birmingham "			10 8						4 45		5 23					
ASHBY dep.			8 22			11 20		1 20			4 10		7 20		7 40		1 35	
Worthington			8 34			11 31		1 32			4 18		7 34		7 52		3 41	
Tonge & Breedon			8 38			11 38		1 38			4 25		7 37		7 57		3 47	
Melbourne			8 48			11 43		1 43			4 30		7 45					
Chellaston & Swarkestone			8 23		8 57		10 35	1 48		1 49	2 12	4 5	4 52	5 47	7 52	7 48	8 20		5 18	
Pear Tree & Normanton			8 29				10 41	1 54		1 55	2 18		4 58		7 57	7 54	8 26			
DERBY arr.			8 35		9 10	10 18	10 48	12 0	12 45	2 8	2 45	8	4 6	5 6	8 9	8 9	8 52		11 58	9 45	7 30

A—Leaves at 9.0 a.m. on Mondays.   B—Fridays excepted.   C—Passengers from Derby arrive at Castle Donington via Trent at 11.18 p.m.
D—On Saturdays leaves Castle Donington at 8.39 and arrives Derby 9.30 p.m.

Passengers holding Season Tickets between Derby & Castle Donington via Chellaston, charged at the ordinary scale, are allowed to travel via Draycott for through purposes only, but are NOT allowed to break their journey at any of the intermediate Stations between Derby & Castle Donington via Draycott.

Midland Railway timetable July–September 1903.

DERBY, MELBOURNE, AND ASHBY.

WEEKDAYS.   **SUNDAYS**

DERBY — dep.	8 30	10 28	13 14	2 38	5 0	5 52	7 22	10 0	5 0	
Pear Tree & Normanton	8 35	10 32	13 18	2 43						
Chellaston & Swarkestone	8 50	10 38	12 52	2 51	5 10	6 0	7 31	10 10	5 10	
Melbourne	8 57	10 44	12 59	3 0	5 16	6 6	7 33	only	5 18	
Tonge & Breedon	9 3	10 49		3 6		6 12	7 43		5 24	
Worthington	9 8	10 55		3 19		6 19	7 48		5 28	
ASHBY — arr.	9 21	11 7		3 27		6 30	8 1			
ASHBY — dep.	8 8	11 14	1 13	3 55		7 8	5 35	
Worthington	8 22	11 27	1 31	4 10		7 21	5 42	
Tonge & Breedon	8 27	11 32	1 36	4 16		7 26	5 47	
Melbourne	8 34	11 37	12 45	1 41	4 25	5 24	7 35	5 53	
Chellaston & Swarkestone	3 40	11 43	12 55	1 47	4 37		7 43	
Pear Tree & Normanton		11 50		1 54	4 44		7 52	
DERBY — arr.	3 48	11 54	1 4	3 0	4 50	5 42	7 57	10 40	To Trent

Does not connect with 5.44 p.m. Derby to Nottingham

Midland Railway timetable July–September 1915.

DERBY, MELBOURNE, AND ASHBY.

WEEKDAYS.   **SUNDAYS.**

DERBY — dep.	8 25	10 20	1 10	2 44	5 53	7 33	10 45	5 0	
Pear Tree & Normanton	8 31	10 25	1 15	2 49		7 44		5 10	
Chellaston & Swarkestone	8 46	10 31	1 21	2 55	6 0	7 52	10 55	5 20	
Melbourne	8 56	10 39	1 29	3 5	6 12	7 32	11 1	5 29	
Tonge & Breedon	9 3	10 44	1 35	3 10	6 19	8 7		5 34	
Worthington	9 8	10 51	1 40	3 20	6 25	8 12		
ASHBY — arr.	9 22	11 4		3 36	6 41	8 17		
ASHBY — dep.	8 2	9 37	11 15	3 57	7 12	5 43	
Worthington	8 15	9 50	11 25	4 12	7 25	5 49	
Tonge & Breedon	8 20	9 55	11 33	4 18	7 30	5 55	
Melbourne	8 27	10 0	11 38	4 27	7 36		
Chellaston & Swarkestone	7 0	8 35	10 7	11 45	4 35	7 45	To
Pear Tree & Normanton		10 13		4 43	7 52	Trent
DERBY — arr.	7 21	8 46	10 22	11 55	4 51	8 5	

Midland Railway timetable October 1921. A selection of passenger timetables for the line.

dominate the goods traffic, milk in particular being an important commodity. Nevertheless, coal from New Lount Colliery and limestone from the Cloud Hill quarry and lime works also formed important workings.

There was a daily goods train to Ashby until 1939, and it is interesting to have a look at details of such a service as documented in Godfrey Yeomans' excellent dissertation (published privately) on the history of the branch. Mr Yeomans records the following details from a Working Timetable for 1st May, 1886.

Apart from alternate Mondays the daily goods was a combined Castle Donington and Ashby working which left Chaddesden Sidings at 7.55 am, arriving at Castle Donington 55 minutes later. Locomotive and brake van then returned to Chellaston to pick up the Melbourne and Ashby traffic and departed Chellaston at 10.05 am. On the return journey the goods left Ashby at 1.05 pm, and arrived Chellaston at 3.10 pm. Twenty minutes later it set off for Castle Donington where it was due to arrive at 3.55. At 4.45 pm it left for Chaddesden Sidings, its booked arrival there being 5.35 pm except on Thursdays when a trip had to be made to Melbourne to pick up fruit and vegetables, the Melbourne-grown produce being in great demand at Derby market on Fridays.

On the alternate Monday the goods left Chaddesden Sidings much later at 10.50 am, and after serving Castle Donington and all stations to Worthington, it stopped at Lount Siding, Heath End, Ticknall Tramway Wharf and Bennett's Brickyard before arriving at Ashby at 3.40 pm. This goods left Ashby at 4.30 pm, and ran directly back to Derby, arriving at Chaddesden Sidings at 6.50 pm.

In the early 1900s the Derby–Ashby branch no longer shared a daily pick-up with the Castle Donington branch, the first rostered goods being the 7.40 am Chaddesden Sidings to Ashby with a return working at 1.45 pm from Ashby. There was also a goods from Chaddesden at 10.20 am that ran to Worthington, its arrival time there being scheduled at 12.25 pm. If it were required to do so, on alternate Mondays locomotive and brake ran forward at 4.30 pm to Ashby to pick up cattle, leaving there 25 minutes later for a return via Worthington to Derby. There were also other variations of time-tabling which are too numerous to merit inclusion in this book which is primarily about the Melbourne Military Railway, but mention must be made of workings in connection with the collieries and the lime-stone quarries.

By the 1930s New Lount Colliery was in full production, consequently Worthington was a very busy station, its services also being required by the Cloud Hill Quarry. The September 1935 Freight Working Timetable is representative of the period. The first train was the 5.30 am Chaddesden to New Lount empties, to be followed ten minutes later by a second train to the same destination. These two trains returned as loaded mineral from New Lount at 7.40 am, and 8.45 am, respectively. The daily goods to Ashby left Chaddesden at 9.20 am, calling as required between Worthington and Ashby before returning at 12.55 pm, from Ashby to Chaddesden. Whenever the colliery or the quarry was very busy an extra train, 1.10 pm from Chaddesden to New Lount, was run when necessary, returning to Derby from New Lount at 2.47 pm. The afternoon empties came out of Chaddesden at 2.32 pm, and the last trip of the day left New Lount Sidings at 4.55 pm.

To complete the story of the line, before turning in detail to the military occupation of the Melbourne branch, it must be stated that normal freight services resumed under LMS control on 1st January, 1945. Traffic to Ashby ceased in 1955 with the abandonment of Ashby Tunnel where the cost of preventing water leakage proved prohibitive. As traffic continued to decline, British Railways found it necessary to close Tonge and Breedon station in September 1959. Worthington was closed in 1964, and Ashby closed down in September 1964 with the end of working on the Ashby–Burton Road section. Melbourne station was closed in July 1965, and Chellaston and Swarkestone in June 1966.

By this time the Melbourne branch, as it was now known, was being worked as a single-shift railway with three return freights, Mondays to Fridays, and one Saturday trip. One of the daily trips was the 7.55 am New Lount Colliery to Drakelow Power Station, the empties returning on the 12 noon Drakelow to New Lount. Coal production ceased at New Lount Colliery in July 1968, and the colliery sidings were taken out of use in November of that year. Derby Power Box came into operation in 1968, and this made manually-operated signal boxes, including all those on the Melbourne branch, redundant. The line was operated from then on as a long siding from Worthington Junction. An occasional trainload of magnesium limestone from Worthington now formed the only traffic, and the revenue from this alone was insufficient to sustain the line. It was finally closed on 21st May, 1980.

As war approached in 1939 it was recognised that the facilities at Longmoor would be inadequate to meet all the needs for training in military railway operations, and the idea for taking over the Melbourne branch of the LMS Railway Company seems to have originated with Colonel Manton, then Principal of the LMS School of Transport at Wilmorton in Derby. Colonel Manton had a long record of service with the Indian Army Engineers, and as a result of his initiative, negotiations were quickly concluded for military occupation of the line from Chellaston East to a point a mile north of Ashby-de-la-Zouch, the military line stopping at that point to avoid complicated level crossings beyond Smisby Road.

Military occupation began on 19th November, 1939 and the line became known as No. 2 Railway Training Centre, Melbourne. Although agreement was reached quickly this might have been because the railway company was not in a strong bargaining position under emergency legislation. Certainly the records of Directors' meetings show clearly considerable resentment of the attitude of the Government on the general question of compensation for requisitioned assets and Government control of the railways. The depth of feeling shared among all the railway companies is shown by Lord Stamp's report to the LMS Board on 17th January, 1940 on the latest discussions between the Government and the railway companies. His report refers to the possibility of action being taken through the Courts or through the House of Commons against the Government, but he suggests that 'it is difficult to take publicly the view that, the Government having now solemnly promised in their scheme to increase rates on lines absolutely agreed by us in order to maintain that revenue and offset increased costs, we disbelieve their bona

The driver of a goods train receiving the tablet authorising him to proceed along the single line section at Melbourne. *Derby Evening Telegraph*

Everything was run according to railway rules when used by the men of the REs as a training depot. This particular scene at Melbourne records men being taken up the line to take up their duties. *Northcliffe Newspapers Ltd*

fides, their intentions or their ability . . . I like less than ever the prospects of litigation or the tender mercies of the House . . .' He recommended, therefore, that the company should accept the Government's latest proposals however much they were disliked. It hardly seems a basis for good co-operation!

Under the agreement with the LMS it was necessary to maintain goods traffic on the line, and although this complicated the military training requirements, it also gave realistic experience to train crews and other operating staff. At first the Royal Engineers had two main tasks on the Melbourne line:

(i)   to build up the facilities for training purposes, and
(ii) to train as many personnel as possible in all aspects of military railway operating.

The former task involved the construction of facilities not necessary on a small LMS branch line, such as loco sheds and sidings at Quarry Junction; a large marshalling yard at King's Newton; storage sheds ultimately for thousands of tons of railway, dockside and bridging stores, and, of course, accommodation for permanent staff and trainees.

An encampment was constructed at King's Newton with the main camp sited across the River Trent at Weston-on-Trent. The size of the latter task can be judged from the fact that, over the first nine months of the war the combined intake of Melbourne and Longmoor was 800 men each month, the combined establishments including trainees, totalling 15,000. The Melbourne line was worked 24 hours per day from 04.00 hours Monday until all traffic had been cleared on Saturday night, thus giving experience of both day and night operations. Sunday was a rest day, very welcome to men who, in addition to working the line, had to put in a certain amount of drill and rifle practice, especially in the period of possible invasion.

As the Longmoor facilities extended and the numbers entering training declined once the initial needs were met, No. 2 Railway Training Centre was closed in 1941 and all initial training was undertaken at Longmoor. That, however, was not by any means the end of RE involvement at Melbourne for the line now became a Collective Training Wing of the Longmoor Military Railway. Under the new arrangements Longmoor was responsible for initial training of recruits and for the formation of units, while Melbourne took responsibility for unit training in railway construction, maintenance, operating and repair. The course for railway construction units included an additional period at the Railway Bridging School at King's Newton which is described fully in Chapter Four.

One of the earliest arrivals at Melbourne was Sapper W.T. Jepson who was posted in 1940 from the Northamptonshire Regiment. The men were accommodated in civilian billets all over Derby, and they came from all kinds of units, but they had one thing in common: they had all been railwaymen before the war began. They travelled out each day by train from Derby Midland Station to Chellaston Quarry to start work building sidings, a loco shed and associated buildings. During this time the camp-site at Weston was being laid out, and in the early Spring of 1940 the Training Battalion moved into a tented camp at Weston. Shortly after that, work started on

Sappers wearing gas masks and protective clothing carrying out experiments in demolition . . . and repair in a 1942 training session. *Authors' Collection*

King's Newton sidings, but Mr Jepson was posted to 191 Railway Operating Company as a steam locomotive driver. 191 Company returned briefly to Melbourne in 1941 to find all the tents replaced by Nissen huts and brick buildings. They returned again in 1942 prior to embarkation for India where they took over the running of the docks at Chittagong, and also worked the Bengal–Assam Railway until the end of the war.

Another early arrival was Ted Baller. Ted was 'called up' from the Great Western Railway Company to the Royal Artillery, with five of his colleagues. The rule was that railwaymen had to be transferred to the Corps of Royal Engineers by 1st April, 1940 or returned to their civilian occupations. On 31st March, 1940 Ted was still with the Royal Artillery.

'They had to get me within twenty-four hours or I went back to Civvy Street,' says Ted. 'I didn't know that, unfortunately. I'd been out shooting all day. I was at Bude in Cornwall, and I was due for a bath that night 'cos we were allocated a bath once a week. We were in a house, sixty of us. All we had was candles, and they said, "Come on. Hurry up. Get your meal; you've got to catch the 6.57. It's the last train out of Bude."

"What for?" we asked.

"Oh, you're going to the Engineers at Derby."

I didn't know quite what . . . you know . . . and when I finally went home on leave I found I was the only so-and-so not back in Civvy Street.'

Arriving at the Drill Hall in Siddals Road, Derby, Ted found men from 'literally hundreds of different regiments' who had been transferred as he had. From Siddals Road he and his fellows marched to Weston Camp, 'because,' says Ted, 'we couldn't get a b..... lorry. Took us hours and hours . . .' When they arrived at Weston, tired after the distance they had marched, carrying full packs and blankets, they found that they had to pitch their tents. There was only one tap in the middle of the field, and this had to provide water for all purposes including the cook-house. The other urgent job was to dig slit trenches in case of air attack, and later they spent their time 'on fatigues' carrying sleepers to build the Quarry Sidings.

George Williams arrived at Weston in June 1940 by a somewhat different route from that of Ted Baller. George had worked as a fireman on the LMS, but joined the Lincolnshire Regiment as a 'Militia Boy' under the 1939 Militia Act. He went to Norway with the BEF as an infantryman, and on evacuation from Norway he was given the choice of returning to Civvy Street as a fireman or joining the RE. He chose the latter, was posted to Weston and then went to the Railway College at Derby where he became an engine driver A3.

George recalls a Merryweather pump installed near Worthington to pump water from the stream into the overhead tank for watering locomotives, and he also recounts the interesting relationship between officers and men working on the line. On one occasion he was working a locomotive with a Second Lieutenant as fireman. George was on 'jankers' for a week for having been A.W.O.L. (Absent without leave) and when the officer joined him on the footplate for duty he said, 'I hope you're not going to take it out on me because you're on "jankers".' On railway duty everyone reverted to his civilian status. A driver or a station master might be a Sapper or an NCO or there might be a Sapper driver and a Corporal fireman on the footplate.

For a locomotive driver the descent from New Lount Colliery to Worthington was the most memorable feature of the line. Using 0−6−0 tank engines 12 to 15 loaded wagons could be brought down from the colliery, but half of them must have their brake levers pinned down in order to negotiate the descent safely.

This descent from New Lount stays in the memory of Mr G.R. Bragg, a civilian shunter who joined the RE at Chester and arrived at Weston in April 1942. By then the RE were operating a Vulcan diesel as well as steam engines. This could take a train of seven or eight wagons down the incline provided that most had their brakes pinned down. If the brakes were not pinned down properly the results could be spectacular − or disastrous − depending on where you stood! On one occasion, for example, a train of 45 wagons stopped at Worthington where *all* the brakes should have been pinned down while the locomotive went off to Cloud Hill to fetch wagons loaded with stone.

The procedure then was for the locomotive with the stone wagons to back on to the waiting trucks, the brakes were picked up and away. This time, however, not all the brakes were pinned down, and as the engine chugged off to Cloud Hill the wagons set off on their own − through Tonge and Breedon, through Melbourne to stop eventually on the viaduct near Quarry Junction, a distance of about nine miles. Fortunately, on this occasion no one was hurt as a result of the lapse in procedures.

It was not always the wagon brakes which caused trouble, however. George Williams recalls that Westinghouse brakes were fitted to the locomotives on the line. They were fitted to give crews experience in their working, but their origin and age were a mystery. These old brake units created a lot of excitement. 'They were very old, and we were very young,' as George Williams put it. It was often necessary to take a spanner, leave the cab and walk along the running plate to give the pump unit a hefty whack to get it working again. This could be quite thrilling with a train of loaded coal wagons on the incline, and it didn't always work − one young Scottish driver finished up with his train on the face of the quarry at Worthington.

Tonge and Breedon station was not far from the pre-war Donington Park motor-racing circuit − now rebuilt and once more open for major motor-racing and motor-cycle racing events. At that time the land was being used by the REME, and tanks, lorries and various tracked vehicles were stored there. These would be loaded on to flat wagons at Tonge for conveyance out to the main line.

Close by Melbourne station was the base for the construction units, and from here had been constructed a suspension bridge of ropes and planks which was used by men crossing the River Trent between Weston Camp and King's Newton base. Mr G.R. Bragg once tried it and found the experience far from pleasant especially if the bridge started to swing, and men not infrequently caused it to do so in moments of high spirits. 'It was,' says Mr Bragg, 'not an experience I should like to repeat.' American engineers probably shared this feeling later.

A more enjoyable experience was the weekend trip into Derby, sometimes behind 'Calder's Taxi'. This was a GWR tender engine, probably a Dean

Activity in the marshalling yard as a heavy crane lifts the jib of a smaller crane during the construction by the men of the R.E. The cranes were used to facilitate the transfer of merchandise arriving at King's Newton.

Northcliffe Newspapers Ltd

Industrial Brownhoist Corporation crane as brought back from Dunkirk by the REs seen here at King's Newton.

R.C. Riley Collection

Further construction work at King's Newton with clearance of the ground for new sidings. The locomotive, No. 7055, is standing on temporary track.

Northcliffe Newspapapers Ltd

Goods which was based at Quarry under the control of a certain Captain Calder. At weekends it was 'bulled up' and attached to a coach to take the men into Derby. It would return from the town at about 23.00 hours making a much faster run than on its outward trip, and 'with everyone on board, including the driver and fireman, pretty well tanked up,' as one old soldier commented. Steven Perceval was, at this time, a goods guard on the LMS, and he was often the guard on trains taken to Quarry by LMS staff to be handed over to the military. Early in the war LMS staff manned the 'Weekend Specials', and he recalls that if the train were stopped short of the station by signals at Derby, the men would leave the train anyway, jumping down and scrambling across the tracks, eager to enjoy the delights of the night life in wartime Derby.

Ted Baller was on duty as Line Inspector one Saturday night when someone pulled the communication cord and stopped the train right across the junction at Chellaston. 'Well,' said Ted, 'the first thing you do is jump down and look for the butterfly on the end of the coach, and you've got him. You turn the butterfly back straight away to get the bloody train off the junction, but then, of course, you couldn't catch the chap because it was non-corridor stock.'

Another interesting week-end working was what, according to Ken Smethurst, was called 'Colonel Manton's Bluebell Party'. This was a Saturday working in which the Engineering Inspector's coach – 'all glass' – was propelled by a loco up to the Ashby end of the line. Sometimes, however, a Drury car was used to take about six people up the line.

The Royal Engineers at Melbourne were able to use the facilities of the LMS School of Transport at Wilmorton in Derby – now British Rail's Engineering School. Colonel Manton had become Principal of the School on its opening in 1936, and one of the superb facilities provided there was an 'O' gauge model railway in the main hall, run in accordance with LMS operating instructions. This was a magnificent model designed with the advice of Sir William Stanier, chief mechanical engineer of the LMS until 1944. The *Derby Evening Telegraph* of 18th September, 1940 carried photographs and a report on the training of REs at the School of Transport:

> In a long hall, the floor of which was sunk resembling in effect a swimming bath, classes were receiving instruction in the operation of signals. For demonstration purposes a wonderfully designed miniature railway ran right round the hall.
>
> Toy trains, worked by electricity, were running on the tracks and the classes were keenly watching the instructor as he switched them from line to line by moving tiny levers.
>
> There was every kind of signal to be seen on a real railway, together with gradient markings, locomotive sheds, turntables and telephones. The signal boxes were exact replicas of those at well-known junctions and there were real block instruments and signal diagrams.

The reporter went on to explain that after three weeks here, the recruits passed on to a 'real railway line which the Engineers have constructed in the country some miles away'. He concluded his report with the comment that courses had been planned 'so that there shall be no waste of time, and so that the greatest possible amount of instruction shall be compressed into the

Many a schoolboy's eyes would sparkle if they could have taken charge of this fine Bassett-Lowke model railway at Derby, used for training the REs.

Northcliffe Newspapers Ltd

shortest period practicable.' The model railway at the School of Transport undoubtedly made a significant contribution to achieving this objective, but not everyone was completely impressed by it.

Brigadier J.C.B. Wakeford has referred to it as 'Colonel Manton's over-elaborate model railway'. He explains further that between the wars he commanded the Rhine Railway Company in Cologne and later in Weisbaden with Captain L. Manton serving under him. Their job was to keep open the line of communication between Cologne and Aachen with only 25 men. To help teach block working by telephone and ticket, Brigadier Wakeford made a simple model: the train was a child's toy, motive power being provided by a push from the instructor's swagger stick; a section was about three feet long, and the whole procedure from 'Can you accept . . .?' to 'Train on line' took about five minutes 'or longer if the learners were a bit stupid.' It was elementary but effective.

In 1927 Brigadier Wakeford went to Longmoor as OC 10th Company, and in the Longmoor workshops he had a similar model built. When war was clearly approaching, an addition to the model was made in the form of French signals and instructions in Continental block working. Again, they were simple, cheap and effective.

When the LMS was setting up the School of Transport at Derby the company provided cash to set up an elaborate model in the main hall. It was electrically powered and built by Bassett-Lowke. If it was required for instructional purposes, several days' notice had to be given to Derby Loco Works who would then send a 'team of cleaners, electricians, etc.,' to prepare the model and to be on hand whilst it was in use. It was not entirely successful as an instructional model for the electrical contacts were too accident-prone, and the sections were too short for the signalling require-ments. Brigadier Wakeford concluded, 'The whole thing was elaborate and expensive . . . but it looked lovely.' This last point can be judged from the photograph on page 45. Sadly, the whole layout was destroyed when it was no longer required for instructional purposes, and the area of the hall once occupied by this 'over-elaborate' model railway is now used as additional office space.

To return to the equipment of the Melbourne Military Railway itself, at the outset it had six LNER 'J69' 0–6–0 tanks and eight corridor coaches from the LMS, still in company livery. From Longmoor there were three ex-GWR coaches, but all of this was transferred from Melbourne when the training requirement changed in 1941. Until then a passenger service had run from Quarry to Smisby Road, rather like the Longmoor 'Bullet'.

At first LMS personnel worked goods trains along the military line, but from May 1940, as military traffic increased, the RE took over complete working of the line, civilian goods being handed over to the LMS at Quarry Junction. To increase their goods-handling capacity the LMS hired six of their class '1F' 0–6–0 tanks which could cope with empty wagons up the 1 in 60 incline out of Worthington more easily than the LNER 'J69s' could.

As has been said earlier, the descent from Lount Colliery was another matter. Crews had to be sure of the right of way through to Tonge before

A general view of the construction of the new marshalling yards at King's Newton by the REs in September 1940. Even fencing was being installed to enclose the yard.

Northcliffe Newspapers Ltd

A close-up of a squad of sappers preparing the 'road' before the ballast is added during training sessions at King's Newton Depot, in September 1940.

Northcliffe Newspapers Ltd

setting out, and on reaching Worthington tickets had to be exchanged with the blockman whilst the train was on the move as it was often very difficult to stop.

A variety of other stock was in use or in store on the line during military occupation, but among the best-remembered were the 0–6–0 tank locomotives brought to Melbourne on lend-lease from the USA. Alterations had to be made to these – both at Derby Works and at Quarry shed – to bring them into line with British and European working practices; repairs to damage caused by sea water during transit from the USA had to be effected as well as repairs just simply to put the locomotives into working order, for it had to be admitted that there were some very old engines among them. Any US locomotive leaving the Melbourne line to travel to its new depot had to have the cabside handrails removed as, with them in place, the locos were ½in. outside the LMS gauge on each side.

These American engines were often cursed by the fitters who had to work on them, especially the earliest arrivals which came without any maintenance guides and were frequently in poor condition. Once in steam and on the road, however, they were generally liked by the engine crews. Mr G.R. Bragg affirmed that they were excellent shunters and performed well the jobs for which they were designed, the main criticisms deriving from their being used for purposes for which they were never intended. He does tell, however, of a little trouble experienced with one of the American locomotives. A Sergeant Instructor was demonstrating the operation of the ratchet regulator fitted to the engine which was standing in Quarry engine shed. Unfortunately, the regulator jammed opened and the locomotive burst through the shed end.

As mentioned earlier, it was necessary to maintain freight traffic on the line so far as was commensurate with military training and the building up of military supplies. Coal was carried from Lount Colliery, earthenware pipes from Lount Pipe-works and limestone from Cloud Hill Quarry. There was also regular traffic serving the market gardens around Melbourne and King's Newton. Ted Baller remembers, for instance, a perishables van being picked up every night at Melbourne for delivery to Chesterfield.

Sid Arkell, who was responsible for much of the commercial traffic at King's Newton, recalls that at night time it was not unknown for tractors to disappear from the depot. He reminisces, 'It was a hell of a big place. They put a guard on one night, but it was hopeless to try to contain the whole depot, and we had a couple of tractors whipped right from under our noses.' At the other end of the commodity scale, Sid remembers that 'thousands and thousands of "Park Drives" were whipped out of the sidings.'

As the Second Front approached thousands of tons of supplies passed through the yard at Quarry and King's Newton, 12-hour shifts frequently being worked to keep military supplies on the move, quite apart from the civilian traffic which, according to Sid Arkell, included a nightly train from Wirksworth to Corby. Presumably, this was carrying limestone from the quarries around Wirksworth to the iron-making blast furnaces at Corby, but it seems a curious working as there was no road through from King's Newton.

As we say in Chapter Seven, the lingering memories of service at Melbourne, as at Longmoor, tend to be happy ones. There were, though, the sad times. Ken Smethurst vividly recalls an accident on the line in which one man was killed and another seriously injured. One early morning in 1940 a Lance-Corporal was waiting at Quarry to signal in a light engine from Melbourne. He was apparently talking to a Sapper and failed either to see or hear the approaching locomotive. To quote Ken:

> They're heavy things, clanking away and all that, but it's a surprising thing that, if the wind's blowing the opposite way, you can't hear them . . . and these two chaps must've been talking, and it ran straight over 'em. The Lance-Corporal, when I got there, they'd already got him laid out on a door in the shunter's room . . . they'd taken the door off and laid him on it. His arm was hanging off . . . and he was begging 'em to shoot him. He was in such a state. The wheels had probably gone right over his arm. They took him to hospital, but before he got there, he died. I went to see the other lad in hospital because I'd known him before the war. I walked straight by his bed; I didn't recognise him, he were such a mess. But he got over it and came back.

Another Royal Engineer was killed when he was thrown from a lorry as it went over a hump-backed bridge in Weston-on-Trent. He'd accepted a lift on an LMS parcels lorry, but he had not been prepared for the bridge.

The greatest collective tragedy at Weston Camp resulted from an attack by a lone German bomber early in the war. On the morning of 11th July, 1940 the night shift had just gone to bed, many in temporary quarters in a marquee, when a German aircraft came in low, dropped its bomb-load on what was fairly obviously a military camp, and disappeared. The marquee was hit and ten men were killed. One had a lucky escape for shrapnel riddled the suitcase lodged under his low camp-bed, but he was completely unhurt.

Although there were no further fatalities from enemy bombing, the Melbourne area does seem to have been a fairly frequent target for attack. It is one of the minor mysteries of the war that the great engineering centre of Derby was never seriously attacked, and various reasons have been suggested for this.

Clive Hardy and Russ Brown in *Derby at War* show that the Luftwaffe maps of the town were obsolete, and R.V. Jones in *Most Secret War* tells graphically how the German bomber-directing radio beams were found targeted on Derby. There is some evidence that afterwards bombs intended for Derby and Nottingham fell, instead, away from those towns. Whether through that, or simply through the existence of a military camp and railway yards, the Melbourne area was bombed on several occasions. Ken Smethurst was on duty in the Control Room at Quarry during one raid. Incendiary bombs were dropped and also high-explosive bombs as a train was on the line to Quarry. 'When the driver got there,' said Ken, 'he reported that there was an S-bend in an otherwise straight line, and he'd never come off the road; he'd come straight through like that.'

Three fine views taken by the model company Bassett-Lowke of Northampton showing their beautiful model of a bridge used for training purposes. Note the line of wagons behind the men. These wagons were models of the special train to take the parts (*see page 54*).

Chapter Four

'Give a Little Whistle'
(The King's Newton Bridging School)

Introducing his fascinating account of the Special Air Service in his book *Who Dares Wins*, Tony Geraghty gives a brief account of the work of the SAS in Europe in 1944. Parties were sent out from Britain to harass enemy communications: roads were mined, railways blown up, and bombing targets reported to the RAF. One SAS-directed attack by the Maquis ended in the destruction of a train carrying 100,000 gallons of petrol. Allied bombers, early in 1944, aimed to isolate Normandy and prevent the Germans sending reinforcements, so bridges across the Seine, railway yards and other facilities were destroyed and the SAS were often involved in pin-pointing targets. In this way the SAS made their particular contribution to the success of the allied invasion of Europe in the summer of 1944. The job of the Royal Engineers was to rebuild these broken communications as soon as possible, and without *their* contribution the successes of D-Day could not have been exploited as they were.

The Manual for the Officers' Bridging Course in 1944 defines military railways bridging as 'The means employed to overcome "obstacles" or "breaches" in the physical line which would otherwise render it useless as an L. of C. (Line of Communication). The Railway Bridging problem is then to provide for the maintenance of the most vulnerable part of L. of C.' Speed was, of course, of the essence in maintaining communications. Delay in the construction of a bridge could turn possible victory to certain defeat. The responsible officer must be able to 'visualise the construction work from beginning to end, recognise and solve problems before the practical work is affected by them, delegate authority as far as possible to his subordinates, keep supplies of materials arriving at the correct time, organise layout of work and stores, see the necessity for safety precautions, and keep his men in good condition physically and mentally.'

Two particular warnings to Bridging Officers are given in the 1944 Manual. One is in the form of an extract from a report on railway and Bridging work in North Africa:

> Very often if a job cannot be done quickly it is not worth doing at all. Junior officers will frequently find themselves in a position where time will not permit reference for decisions to higher authority. They must be trained to be capable of taking important decisions, and to force a job through with aggressive determination. At the same time officers must be trained to make brief but complete and accurate and *above all* speedy reports.
>
> However, care must be taken when assessing damage. A 'civilian source' is quoted on damaged bridges: 'It was found that reports of damage tended to be greatly exaggerated and the co-efficient of exaggeration was about 85 per cent'.

To provide the necessary training for officers and men a Bridging School was opened at King's Newton, soon after military occupation of the Melbourne line. Known as No. 926 Railway Bridging Company at No. 2 ETC Melbourne, it was the only such training establishment in the country. All British Railway Construction Companies passed through the King's Newton courses, the bridging course being concentrated into four to five weeks, operating courses slightly longer. Demolition courses were carried out mainly at Longmoor. Although there were staff exchanges between Melbourne and Longmoor, and frequent cross-postings, Melbourne men looked upon Longmoor as a sort of Siberian exile.

A typical Bridging Course would be constituted as follows:

Week 1 – Rigging and Steel Derricks
Week 2 – Foundations and Piers
Week 3 – Bridge Calculations and Standard Railway Bridging
Week 4 – Standard Bridging and Repairs to Damaged Bridges
Week 5 – Repairs to Damaged Bridges

A detailed timetable was produced for each week and set out below are the instructions for the Field Ropeway Project of 15th January, 1944.

Officers Railway Bridging Course No. 5
Field Ropeway Project

1. *Object*
To practice officers in calculation, using Field Formulae.

2. *Situation*
An imaginary bridge on the Low Level Site has been destroyed. It is required to build a temporary bridge as soon as possible. This involves at least two approach spans on the North Bank.

3. *Narrative*
A reconnaissance has been made and it has been decided that the approach spans on the far bank will consist of R.S.J. spans N-26 on 'L' Trestling Piers.

It is proposed that the Stores be conveyed to the far bank by means of a Field Ropeway.

Stores available for Field Ropeway.
Up to 25' Spars.
2½" S.W.R.
23 No. 5 ft. Pickets.
Sleepers.
Ample supply of blocks, cordage, etc.

4. *Requirement I*
As No. 2 Section Officers, XXX R.C. Coy., R.E.
(a) Inspect the site.
(b) Submit detailed calculations and sketches for the Field Ropeway by 09.00 hrs 14 Jan.44.

5. *Requirement II*
Construct the Field Ropeway on 15 Jan.44.
Convey one N-26 across the gap and back and dismantle ropeway.

6. *General Instructions*
(a) Restrictions – Existing bridges and floating craft will NOT be used to convey erection stores across the gap.
(b) Discipline – Work on Saturday, 15 Jan.44 will continue until the job has been completed to the satisfaction of Officer i/c Rigging. This will include dismantling.
(c) Officer i/c Erection – LIEUT TREADGOLD, P.H., R.E.
(d) Messing – The Officer i/c Erection will be responsible for arranging meals with the Messing Officer. Meals will not be served at King's Newton on Saturday, 15 Jan.44.

Bridging School,
C.T.W., Tn.T.C., R.E.

Capt. R.E.,
for Major R.E.,
Instructor, Bridging.

Note that work was to continue until the project was completed *and* dismantled. Each company, during its course at King's Newton, was required to construct a low-level bridge across the River Trent in both daytime and night-time conditions. Although units also practised the erection of suspension bridges for pedestrians, the 'swinging bridge' – remembered with little affection by many who used it – was a semi-permanent feature of the Weston-Melbourne-King's Newton camp. It was designed and built to ease communication between the encampments north and south of the river, but there were those who preferred to take the long way round after trying it once.

The training courses laid emphasis on the need to use local resources as far as possible in bridge-building and repair, but there were, of course, items of standard equipment which companies could hope to use. These included various types of trestle, both timber and metal, R.S.J. bridge spans, welded sectional bridges and lattice-girder spans. However, the most important contribution of King's Newton to bridge design was the development of the Unit Construction Railway Bridge (UCRB). This was designed under the leadership of Lt Colonel Everall whose work has received *less* than its deserved recognition. 'Bailey' bridges for military and civilian use are well known, but they were designed for road traffic including heavy armoured vehicles. Such bridges were tested for railway use at King's Newton, but to erect them for locomotive use proved a complicated task, and the bridges suffered alarming deflections under the weight of locomotives. Lt Colonel Everall, a former Chief Engineer of Indian Railways and an Indian Army Officer, was required to design bridging units to meet the following conditions:

(a) To give an assembly requirement at site which was as simple as possible, permitting it to be erected if necessary at night, and at all times without cranes.
(b) Absolute inter-changeability of the individual pre-fabricated members was required.
(c) The design of the individual members was such that they could be easily transported by road or rail, and could be handled by manpower, or at least without the use of a power-operated crane.
(d) The plate girder bridges did not allow very much flexibility in the selection of spans. It was desired, in the UCRB equipment, to produce such a range of members that a greater flexibility in the selection of spans was possible.
(e) The members were designed so that the erection of both deck and through type bridges, either square or skew, was possible.
(f) To ensure that the equipment could be used in practically any theatre of operations, it was desired to make it capable of carrying various loadings and a range of permanent gauges.

Initially spans of up to 75 ft were provided, but subsequently spans of 120 ft and 150 ft were produced. These designs proved very effective in war conditions and the photographs on *pages 55, 81 and 82*, show them in use.

For training purposes, Bassett-Lowke made a superb model of the bridging equipment and this facility was installed at King's Newton as shown on *page 50*. Because it was produced for specialist railway purposes, the Everall Unit Construction Railway Bridge did not become as popularly

TRAIN LOADING DIAGRAM FOR TYPICAL HIGH LEVEL SCHEME

C · U · R · B

NE: THIS DIAGRAM IS INTENDED TO SHEW THE ORDER IN WHICH MATERIAL SHOULD ARRIVE AT THE SITE IT GIVES *NO* INDICATION OF THE LOADING CAPACITY OF WAGONS NOR IS IT AN ACCURATE MATERIAL LIST

FIRST TRAIN — Light Standard Steel Trestle Units etc for Piers & Erection Gantries

Each wagon unloaded as near bridge site as possible

10T WAGON	10T WAGON	40' FLAT	40' FLAT	4 20' FLAT	40 FLAT	40' FLAT	40' FLAT	1 40' FLAT
Columns L 4	Columns L 2 & L 3	Columns L 1	Columns L 9	Joists L 9	Joists L 8 & N 25 (for Floating Gantry)	Mk V Pontoons	Mk V Pontoons	Mk V Pontoons

TO BRIDGE SITE

10T WAGON	10T WAGON	10T WAGON	10T WAGON	10T WAGON	10T WAGON	10T WAGON	9 10T WAGON	10T WAGON
Cover Plates, Clips, Bolts, Etc	Chain Blocks S.W.R. Cordage Jacks Etc	Launching Rollers Side Guide Rollers	Camels Feet	Camels Feet	Driving Tubes, Capstans Etc V 31, V32, V 33A, V 34	Angle Bracings L 17 Stools L 35	Tubular Bracings L 6 & L 7 (L 56 & L 51)	Tubular Bracings (L 56 & L 51)

SECOND TRAIN — UCRB Units for 2/65ft & 2 75ft Spans with Launching Equipment

Wagons unloaded alongside track in the relative position shown below

TO BRIDGE SITE

40' FLAT	10T WAGON 20' FLAT	10T WAGON 20' FLAT	4 40' FLAT	40' FLAT	3 40' FLAT	40' FLAT	1 20' FLAT
16 Erection Trolleys	Cross Frames Bed Plates Bolts	Cross Frames 2 Winches Bed Plates S.N.R. Bolts Blocks Jacks Etc	16 20' Chord Units 5 Verticals, 32 Diagonals 4 End Posts Spikes & Bearings	16 15' Chord Units 16 10' Chord Units 76 Verticals, 28 Diagonals 4 End Posts Splices & Bearings	8 15' Chord Units 14 15' Chord Units 19 Verticals, 70 Diagonals 4 End Posts Splices & Bearings	8 End Posts 14 15' Chord Units Splices & Bearings	1 Section Launching Nose

DRAWING 1

This diagram is a reproduction from the original document intending to show the order in which the material should arrive at the site of the bridge construction.

This picture shows the way a derrick was made and used in bridge construction.

Authors' Collection

Two LMS class '4Fs' seen here speeding at 40 mph over a temporary bridge constructed at King's Newton in March 1942; the Army officers are watching the deflections.

Authors' Collection

The suspension bridge constructed by the REs to link Weston camp with the King's Newton Depot. This crossed the River Trent and the men used it four times a day to and from duty.   *Authors' Collection*

Sappers being trained in boiler-tube replacement using old loco boilers at King's Newton in September 1940.   *Derby Evening Telegraph*

known as the Bailey bridge, but it was equally vital to the successful pursuit of the war. Derivatives of the UCRB can be seen today supporting bridges under repair on modern motorways – a latter-day example of 'giving aid and comfort to the enemy!'

Training was also given in the use of cranes, derricks and joists. For this purpose several types of crane were in use at King's Newton including one 36-ton crane. The first crane at Melbourne was a Brown hoist brought back from France in the evacuation of the BEF at Dunkirk. This hoist was of American origin and it arrived packed in crates with no drawing or instructions for erection. The giant Meccano puzzle was eventually solved, and the much-travelled hoist was put into use along the line. That was not, however, the end of the saga, for on one occasion the crane came off the main line, slid down the banking and finished up on its side at the bottom.

There were other occasions when all did not go as planned. It was the practice at King's Newton to demonstrate the effect of explosives by blowing branches off trees. Ken Hicklin tells how one day a mistake was made and no tamping was used. The resulting explosion blew out all the windows at a nearby farm. Glass, like many other commodities, was not easily obtainable at that time, but all the windows were replaced by nightfall. Ken and the farmer are still neighbours, but Ken is not allowed to forget this little act of inadvertent vandalism.

Some of the work in north-west Europe of graduates of the King's Newton Bridging School is shown in *Chapter Six*.

Bridge training over the Trent with a Low-level bridge being assembled by the REs in May 1942.	*Authors' Collection*

Two further views of the bridge exercise in May 1942. Note the Melbourne Line in the top left of the upper view. *Authors' Collection*

Chapter Five
'American Patrol'
(North American Railwaymen in Britain and Europe)

761st Railway Transportation Company

As with most aspects of World War II American units played a role which grew steadily in size and importance from 1942 until by D-Day American strength was pre-dominant.

The first American railway unit to arrive in Britain was the 761st Railway Transportation Company; indeed, it was the first American railway unit to serve overseas anywhere in World War II. The 761st was activated at Camp Shelby, Mississippi on 29th June, 1942 with Capt. Christopher H. Anderson as company commander. All personnel had worked on civilian railways before joining the army, and had received basic and technical training with their former units – the 711th, 713th and 727th Engineer Railway Operating Battalions. As the 761st they comprised 50 yard crews to work in marshalling yards.

On 31st August, 1942 the 761st sailed from New York aboard the *Queen Elizabeth* and arrived in Greenock on 5th September. They left immediately for Weston-on-Trent. During their time at Weston they received technical training on European equipment with the LMS and worked the Melbourne Military Railway.

The 761st had been formed to handle rail movements of Air Corps equipment to various bases in England, and worked closely with Royal Engineers. A British view of this developing alliance has been given by Mr G.R. Bragg, then a Sapper with the RE. In July 1942 a detachment from 181 Company, RE was sent to a tented camp at Marchington, a village on the Uttoxeter side of Derby. Sapper Bragg felt that this camp was appropriately named for each morning they were marched to Sudbury where they assisted in preparing a camp for American engineers. At that time No. 600 Construction Company was being prepared for active service overseas and life was hectic: reveille at 04.30 hours and work on 12-hour shifts. 'Horrible! But it really kept you fit,' said Mr Bragg.

At Sudbury there were 12 big rail sidings, each holding about 100 wagons. Beyer-Garrett locomotives would arrive with about 100 empty wagons to be loaded with rubble, or full of ashes to be unloaded. Off this yard was laid a great circle of track which encompassed several farms. When the circle was complete, dead-end sidings were constructed at intervals, and at the end of each siding were Nissen huts holding aircraft parts, ammunition or bombs. When all this was completed the camp was occupied by American units of which 761st RTC was the first.

The arrival of the American units had its amusing side. American shunters did not use shunting poles and were not familiar with fly-shunting. When they saw it they were amazed, but liked what they saw and determined to try it, with the result that a good many coal wagons were run off the road, but they became used to it. The great circle of railway track had the effect of isolating some four or five farms. Unable to get their milk away from the farms, the farmers adopted the practice of stopping the American trains and loading their churns on to flat wagons until proper crossings were built – an unusual but effective example of Anglo-American co-operation.

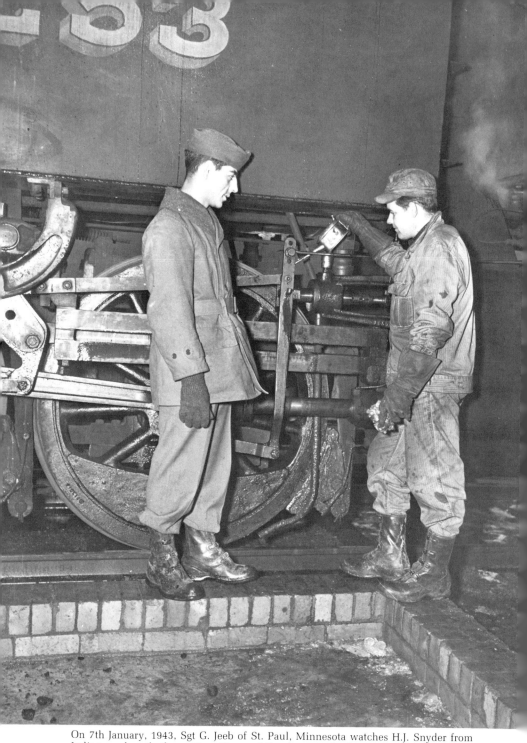

On 7th January, 1943, Sgt G. Jeeb of St. Paul, Minnesota watches H.J. Snyder from Indiana as he oils the motion. Corporal Snyder was the first American serviceman to qualify as an engineer in a test given by the British Railway authorities.

U.S. Army Signal Corps

The 761st did not stay very long in England, nor did they remain handling aircraft parts. The unit was chosen to participate in the invasion of North Africa, one detachment leaving Liverpool aboard the *U.S.S. Uruguay* and another leaving Greenock aboard *S.S. Empress of Canada* on 31st October, 1942, landing in Oran, Algeria on 11th November, 1942. There they worked as stevedores and RTOs, and handled train movements at the docks. They also operated ammunition and supply trains as far as Souk-el-Arba, Tunisia to the east, and southerly to Colum Bachor in French Morocco. When the fighting had moved on the 761st operated railways from Oran to Algiers and from Oran to Oujola in French Morocco. Finally, in the words of Sgt Harry R. McLaughlin, 'After nineteen months of combatting the enemy, the Arabs, antique French engines, the chef du gars, the grasshopper plague and the steep grades in the mountains, preparations were made for movement to Italy.'

After sailing to Naples in June 1944 the unit worked rail lines in and around Naples and Salerno. With only limited track available, and with antiquated steam locomotives they moved a greater tonnage of goods through Naples than passed through the port of New York in the same period.

In December 1944 they moved on to Marseilles, and on Christmas Day, 1944 arrived in Sarrebourg, Lorraine. From there they moved progressively to Kaisers-lautern, Ludwigshafen, and on 6th May, 1945 to Munich where they were based on VE day. From Munich they ran trains through Innsbrück and the Brenner Pass to Northern Italy until July 1945 when the 761st was broken up.

Other detachments of American units continued to visit Longmoor and Melbourne, along with Canadians, Australians and others, but it was in 1944 that the American presence was felt in strength.

755th Railway Shop Battalion

This battalion was first constituted as the 662nd Engineer Battalion in 1933, but was re-activated as 755th Railway Shop Battalion on 20th November, 1942 at Camp Clairborne, Louisiana. On 5th November, 1942 all Engineer Railway units were transferred from the Corps of Engineers to the Transportation Corps and the word 'Engineer' was dropped from the designation. A similar change was made in Britain much later with not a little heart-searching by the Royal Engineers.

The Norfolk & Western Railroad Company was the sponsor and supplied the Officers to the battalion, the CO being Lt Col Miles G. Stevens of Georgia. The 755th was organised to repair railway equipment and included all necessary personnel to effect the building and repair of locomotives, wagons (cars) and to work any railway equipment. It was, in fact, equipped to carry out heavier repairs than any other unit.

'A' Company comprised an erecting shop platoon, a machine shop platoon and a diesel-electric platoon. Its function was to strip locomotives for repair, performing machining operations on steam and diesel-electric locomotives as well as on steam cranes.

'B' Company was a Boiler and Smith Shop Company whose function was to repair locomotive boilers and tanks, and to do all work relating to plate, sheet metal and structural work, forgings, springs and pipe fitting. It forged tools and produced brass castings for the battalion.

'C' Company was a Car Repair Company.

After basic training at Clairborne, technical training at Bucyrus, Ohio and on the New York Central Railway system, the battalion moved overseas and arrived at Sudbury, near Derby, on 17th December, 1943. There they erected wagon assembly lines and began to turn out wagons, eventually achieving a production rate of one wagon every 45 minutes. A detachment also went to King's Newton (Weston Camp) where, for a month, they were building American tank cars. A further detachment at Caerphilly was engaged in modifying U.S. type 2–8–0 locomotives to British standards, and servicing Whitcomb 650 hp diesels.

In April 1944 the battalion was given an unusual task. They moved to Truro and Hayle in Cornwall to construct steel oil barges, assisting British civilian contractors who were launching one barge every 10 to 12 days. The 755th were eventually able to launch one barge every 26 hours, and made rapid inroads into the stockpile of material. As the official record states: 'Colonel Stevens had told his men to "run 'em out of steel" and that is exactly what they went ahead and did. In fact, they were running them out of most everything as well.'

On 15th June, 1944 the battalion moved to Longmoor where they were occupied in tasks similar to those carried out at Sudbury and King's Newton, and they achieved similar rates of wagon production. They were also engaged in assembling 15-ton cranes, steam-locomotive cranes of 6 and 10 tons, and in general maintenance and repair of Whitcomb diesels.

Again in January, 1943, servicemen from America employ the 'assembly line' technique of unloading a freight car at King's Newton Depot. *U.S. Army Signal Corps*

The monthly summary of battalion activities for July 1944 shows some of the routine:

HEADQUARTERS

755TH RAILWAY SHOP BATTALION
APO 350   US ARMY

1 August 1944

SUBJECT: History of Unit for July 1944

TO: Commanding General, Forward Echelon Hq, CZ, Transportation Sec. APO 350 US Army

The following events took place during the month of July 1944:

1. 30 EM (over-strength as per T/O 55-235; 44 Oct. 1943) relieved of assigned [sic] & transferred to 756th Ry Shop Bn 4 July 1944
2. Detachment 'A' (Mobile Ry Shop) 1 Officer and 30 EM to Caerphilly for further training. 5 July 1944
3. 3 EM became citizens after being duly sworn at Salisbury. (Pfc. Joe Maldonado, S/Sgt. John Hernandez, and S/Sgt. Vincent A. Birzatiz) 8 July 1944
4. 3 Officers were promoted: 1st Lt. Charles M. Bainbridge to Captain; 2nd Lt. William J. Cadigan to 1st Lt.; and 2nd Lt. Joseph B. Bernard to 1st Lt. 15 Jul.
5. 5 EM were promoted Tec. 5 Emil I. Teghitto to Tec 4; Tec 5 Cyril P. O'Donovan to Tec 4; Private John N. Ware to Tec 5; Pvt. Oscar W Miller to Pfc; and Pvt. Roy M. Knutson to Pfc.
6. Capt. Bainbridge to Ashchurch and Derby for purpose of checking special equipment of unit. 13 July 1944
7. 22 EM (over 5% basic privates) declared over-strength and sent to 10th Replacement Depot at Lichfield. 22 July 1944.
8. 70 EM and one Officer sent to Caerphilly for purpose of assisting other TC units in detail work. 18 July 1944
9. 9 EM attached-unassigned to this unit were relieved of attached-unassigned and transferred to the 756th Ry. Shop Bn.
10. Officers of this unit took a map-reading course at Longmoor (Apple Pie) Camp.
11. Crews of Officers and EM fired the 50 Cal. gun at Winchester, 26 July 1944
12. Men of this unit participated with the British in their Field Day of sports on the 22nd of July 1944. 2 Officers assisted as judges.
13. S.L.O.E. and organizational equipment sent to PE. Equipment at Sudbury departed 24 July 1944; at Honeybourne departed 25 July 1944; and at this station departed 26 July 1944.
14. This unit relieved of assigned to 708th Ry Grand Div. at midnight 31 July 44 and assigned to the 706th Ry Grand Division.
15. The average daily non-effective rate for the first three weeks of month is . . .1.60
16. Lt. Col. Stevens active during the month in connection with Diesel inspections at Weston-on-Trent and Caerphilly as well as actual operations at Longmoor Downs. American-British relations furthered successfully by active participation of this unit with the British in whose camp we have been quartered since 11 June 1944.

During this month the unit as a whole made excellent progress in the production of tank cars, flats, and goods wagons.

For the Commanding Officer:
O.T. Tormoen
Capt.   TC
Unit Historical O.

Three views showing American personnel unloading and assembling box-cars at Weston-on-Trent in 1944.
Authors' Collection

Map-reading courses, experience in firing the 50 calibre AA gun at Winchester, and further training at Caerphilly were all preparatory to the move to the Continent and on 1st August, 1944 the 755th was transferred from the 708th Railway Grand Division to the 706th, prior to moving from Longmoor to Romsey to await transport to the Continent. The official historian comments:

> The time at Longmoor had been utilised to the fullest both as to the work accomplished and the good will established between the British and ourselves.

That last comment was endorsed by REs, who spent that period at Longmoor.

Arriving in France over Utah Beach, the 755th moved on to Rennes to be re-assigned to their old 708th Railway Grand Division, and began the long task of restoring order to railway yards and equipment badly damaged by Allied bombing. By the end of September the Rennes yard was in good order, and the battalion moved on to Belgium. Extracts from the official summary of activities for December 1944 show that 'active military service' had real meaning for the 755th while based at Namur:

2. Captain Frederick Stiff and 1st Lt William O. Hunt, Jnr, went to Valenciennes, France in order to secure quarters for the battalion in case an emergency movement were necessary in connection with the recent German counterattack.

7. Christmas was celebrated with proper services and touches of yuletide spirit wherever possible. The men were given a turkey dinner with all the trimmings. Work schedules went ahead as usual.

8. Strictest enforcement of safety rules was invoked caused by the shift in the fighting front. Guns were placed around the sleeping quarters and an air watch was established at the Namur shops with a G.I. and a civilian always on duty. At Liege, Company 'C' was in the center of numerous buzz-bomb and enemy plane attacks. Private John H. McGillis of that company lost his life through enemy action. At Namur several night attacks were made by enemy planes and several buzz-bombs were sent over.

9. As representative of Brig. General Clarence L. Burpee, Colonel Stevens attended funeral services for a Belgian railroad worker at the Namur shops who had been killed by a flying bomb.

11. During the month of December the following results were obtained at the Namur, Liege (Ans) shops and the Herbesthall roundhouse.

Class 5 Repairs	9
Heavy Run Repairs	82
Heavy Run Repairs (Accident)	13
Lite Run Repairs	23
Total	127

Miscellaneous Car Equipment repaired   1157
(This total is less report from Company 'C'
    for 30th December, 1944)

During von Runstedt's counter-offensive in the autumn of 1944 advance units of the German Army had advanced to within 15 miles of Namur and 20 miles of Liege, and small units had infiltrated Namur itself, but by late

January 1945 the Allied front lines were advancing steadily and von Runstedt's gamble had clearly failed. By early February it was possible for men of the 755th to take day trips to Brussels, and spells of leave in England were organised to the great benefit of battalion morale.

The work of repair and modification went on unabated through February and March: for example, 36 locomotives of the USA 2 – 8 – 0 type had cylinders welded to keep them in service, otherwise lack of spare parts would have kept them dead. From late March activity slackened, but at 31st August, 1945 the official record showed that since the battalion arrived in France on 15th August, 1944 they had repaired and put back into service 647 locomotives and 4,294 cars of all types.

On 8th May the battalion took part in the VE Day Parade through Namur. It had played its part 'in seeing to it that supplies rolled to the First and Ninth Armies when they counted most.'

The official summary also records that in August 1945 three enlisted men of the battalion were married in Namur, thus 'enhancing the "good neighbour" policy.' How neighbourly could you get?

763rd Railway Shops Battalion

This battalion was activated on 27th July, 1943 at New Orleans, Louisiana, and basic training began at Camp Harahan. As the official battalion records says: 'The Mission of the battalion was a technical one. Nevertheless the primary task of the officers and men was military . . . should the occasion arise for the outfit to take part in battle they must be prepared.'

Technical training followed at Camp Millard, Bucyrus, Ohio in October 1943, and on 3rd May, 1944 the battalion left New York aboard the *Athlone Castle*. The unit was sponsored by the Delaware, Lackawanna and Western Railroad Company. On 19th October, 1943 Company President William White wrote to the Commanding Officer of the New Orleans Training Centre after being informed that the 763rd had been rated the highest of any unit that had ever left the centre:

> We never had any doubt that the officer personnel of this battalion would be a credit to the Army, the Lackawanna Railroad and to themselves; but to receive official advice from you as Commanding Officer of the Training Center that this battalion rated so highly is most pleasing. We look for the same results from that battalion when it gets into action.

He was not to be disappointed, but first, the engineers of the 763rd had to zig-zag their way across the North Atlantic. It took twelve days, during which the amateur navigators amongst them imagined themselves all over the globe. They eventually found themselves in Liverpool, England, and on the following day 'A' and 'Hq' companies went to Weston-on-Trent, 'C' company to Sudbury and 'B' company to Hainault near London. For 'A', 'Hq' and 'C' companies it was a far cry indeed from the off-duty pleasures of New Orleans or New York.

The work was somewhat different from that for which they had been trained. A comment from official sources said, 'After all our training in machine shops and engine houses, we were handed a crow-bar and a rivet

Steam up! Steam leaks from a USA 0-6-0 Tank on the Melbourne line on 7th January, 1943 with Private E. Donaldson and Corporal H. Snyder in charge.

U.S.A. Army Signal Corps

The first American railroad crew to run a locomotive on a British main line in January 1943: on the ground (*left*) Corporal Harry Roth, Private James F. Cox and in the cab (*left*) Private Fred. N. Wilkesbarre, Private C. Murphy and Private James Curcio. *U.S. Army Signal Corps*

hammer and set to work assembling boxcars.' 'B' and 'C' companies worked on established assembly lines and built new ones, but at Weston 'A' and 'Hq' companies started from scratch.

Nevertheless, the 763rd enjoyed their stay in 'Merry Old England' and enjoyed good relations with their British counterparts at Weston camp. Some British customs were quickly adopted by the American guests: fish and chips, and 'Another pint o' bitter, dook!' However, life also had its problems like 'negotiating the English countryside with its winding roads and hedged meadows was enough of a problem in daylight, let alone in the darkness of wartime blackout with a full load of "mild and bitters".' Triple summer-time with its 'midnight sunsets' did help, though.

Company 'B' had a harsh reminder of their reason for being in England when a 'buzz-bomb' (V1 Flying Bomb) hit their camp early one morning in July 1944. Fortunately, it fell short of the barracks and there were no casualties.

On completion the box-cars were shipped to the Continent via Southampton. Over 7,000 cars were built that summer by the battalion, but by the end of October a more pressing need was for railroad units on the Continent to maintain communication lines. The Weston car-lines were closed at the end of October, 'A' and 'Hq' companies joining 'C' company at Sudbury. After completing work on the car-lines there, all three companies left Sudbury on 12th November, 1944. 'B' company was to remain at Hainault.

The next few days were not pleasant: three days of dragging their duffle-bags through English mud, then across the Channel to Le Havre where they received the friendly greeting of 'Who the hell are you and where did you come from?' Ignoring hostilities, the 763rd pressed on: '. . . the landing craft grounded on the beach. Bulldozers quickly built a small causeway of sand and off we went, "struggling up the beach-head against heavy opposition" of the unmentionable duffle-bag. The 763rd Railway Shop Battalion had landed on the continent of Europe!' From there they were taken by lorry to a wet, muddy field and ordered to pitch tents. What a contrast to their training camps at New Orleans!

At the end of November they moved to Belgium. While the rest of the battalion stayed at Malines, Warrant Officer 'Jimmy' De Luca went on to Antwerp. He was killed by a V-bomb, and the battalion mourned the loss of a very popular NCO.

'A' and 'Hq' companies moved to Louvain where the yards had been hammered by Allied air forces. Shops, barracks, track, locos and rolling stock had all been smashed. This was a job for which Railway Shop Battalions had been trained, and by mid-January 1945, when they were joined by 'B' company from Hainault, the full strength of the 763rd was concentrated on restoring the facilities at Louvain.

The following extract from the Commendation sent to the 763rd from the Headquarters of the 2nd Military Railway Service in July 1945 sums up their achievement:

> 2.a. The record of operational work completed by your organisation in the performance of its primary mission of repairing and maintaining railway locomotives and cars used for military traffic, and processing and preparing

for service of new locomotives, involving locomotive shop operations at Louvain, Belgium and car shop operations at Antwerp (North Yard), Belgium is very gratifying.

2.b. Your organisation likewise has performed consistently in a most commendable manner in the operation of enginehouses, and in handling car inspection and running repair work at Louvain, Muisen (near Malines) and Ans (near Liege), Belgium; also in the successful accomplishment of numerous special missions comprising various other mechanical and miscellaneous work for which 763rd personnel have been used.

3. The results indicated were achieved under extremely difficult conditions, including exposure to severe enemy action during a substantial part of the period concerned, had required constant hard work and ingenuity on the part of the officer and enlisted personnel, and superior technical qualifications, state of military training and devotion to duty.

Canada declared war on Germany on 10th September, 1939, but Canadian railway units as such did not arrive in Britain until after the first US units. As in Britain, reserves had been run down between the wars, and on the outbreak of war no reserve railway units existed, the reserve Railway Corps having been finally disbanded in 1935.

Railway troops were not among those sent abroad immediately, primarily owing to the need to safeguard rail communications in Canada. It was also policy to send abroad initially only technical units who would directly support Canadian fighting units and not Line of Communication units. This decision was not welcomed in Britain, and repeated requests were made for the Canadians to send railway companies to France up to the time of the evacuation of the BEF. Later, as further pressure grew on Britain's railway resources, requests for assistance were renewed and on 23rd April, 1943 No. 1 Railway Operating Group was formed at Stratford, Ontario for service overseas. The constituent strength of the group was:

	Officers	ORs
H.Q. No. 1 Railway Operating Group	4	24
No. 1 Railway Workshop Company	7	429
No. 1 Railway Operating Company	7	368
No. 2 Railway Operating Company	7	368
H.Q. No. 1 Railway Telegraph Company	1	11
No. 1 Railway Line Maintenance Company	1	51
No. 1 Railway Telegraph Operating Section	1	43
	28	1,294

No. 2 Railway Operating Company was formed in England on 6th May, 1943 and went to Longmoor while No. 1 Railway Operating Company was formed in Canada and received basic military training there before embarking for England. They left Halifax aboard the *Queen Elizabeth* on 23rd July, 1943 and arrived at Gourock on the 28th.

No. 2 Railway Operating Company had, in the meantime, completed initial training at Longmoor, and on 6th August moved to Weston-on-Trent for advanced training. Their place at Longmoor was taken by No. 1 Railway

Operating Company, and training over the next few months involved a good deal of movement around the country as the men familiarised themselves with operating, maintenance and workshop practice at Darlington, Dore, Swindon, Derby and on the Melbourne Military Railway.

By early 1944 Canadian railway engineers were providing assistance throughout the British railway system, primarily as foremen, brakesmen, shunters and loco-shed staff, but later Canadian drivers accompanied their British counterparts on the footplate. The Canadian railmen's introduction to British lines was not always either easy or friendly. The British trades unions objected to the presence of non-union men, and would accept them only as labourers. That difficulty was, however, overcome and the scheme was successful. The Official History says, 'Since most of the men were billeted in the towns, they learned what it was like to live as civilians in wartime England. Many lasting friendships were formed because of mutual railroading interests and not a few marriages were contracted.'

As the build-up to the invasion of Europe continued, men of the Royal Canadian Engineers were sent on courses, mainly at Longmoor, to train on US diesel-electric locomotives which were assigned to France after the invasion, and to learn about French signalling practices. Canadian drivers gaining footplate experience were delighted to have the opportunity to ride such locomotives as *Flying Scotsman* and *Royal Scot*, but it was a mixed pleasure. They missed the powerful headlights of their own engines (which could not have been used in black-out Britain, even if fitted). 'The firemen learned again how back-breaking a task it was to stoke the firebox for a fast express, most having become accustomed to the automatic stokers of Canadian long-distance engines.' It was an important skill to acquire – or to re-acquire – for many British locomotives were destined for use in France.

Workshop Companies continued to be sent to LNER and LMS workshops, but more for work than for training. In March 1944 a 20-man detachment joined the 728th U.S. Railway Operating Battalion on box-car construction at Sudbury near Derby. Finally, in April 1944 all Canadian forces were equipped with British motor vehicles as it was assumed that they would be operating in areas served mainly by RE workshops. The Canadians were not entirely impressed by the British locomotives; they were even less impressed by the British Army motor vehicles. Much later a senior transport officer recalled 'what a constant headache they were . . . I never found out how to keep a motor in the "car, light utility 4 × 2" for much more than 5,000 miles without replacing it. It was indeed a poor substitute for the Willys' Jeep, and this we acquired in due course from the salvage dumps in Normandy.'

The Telegraph Company left for Normandy on 29th July, the two operating companies in August, but No. 1 Railway Workshop Company stayed in England until November. At Sudbury they carried on building box-cars and erected 965 in all, reaching a peak of 16 per day. In October they went to Longmoor to work on locomotives, and assembled 56 before leaving for France on 19th November.

The first duties of the RCE railwaymen in France were to help road movement of stores needed to maintain the rapid advance of the Allied forces. It was not until 8th September, 1944 that they began railway operations when No. 1 Railway Operating Company took responsibility for the line from Lisieux to Elbeuf. No. 2 Railway Operating Company took over the line from Elbeuf to Serqueaux. This line was in poor condition, and the need for major repairs delayed the start of scheduled operating until 24th September. The two companies then rapidly built up their services so that in October they carried 165,104 tons of supplies, using 11,715 wagons of assorted types and origins in 699 trains.

The Official History highlights an unusual problem for transport officers:

> As might be expected, when trains had to be despatched via Paris the greatest problem was getting the crews and engines back from that interesting city, for not only was the city an attraction, but the Americans were naturally only too ready to make use of any locomotives that came their way.

Two engines disappeared on a trip to Paris, and were eventually found after a week's search near Dijon close to the Swiss border.

In February and March 1945 No. 2 Operating Company moved to Nijmegen to prepare for railway operating on the other side of the Rhine. That river was crossed on 23rd March, and in early April No. 2 Operating Company moved to Rheine on the River Ems to begin operating the line from Emmerich to Rheine. Shortly afterwards No. 1 Operating Company took control of the line from Rheine to Kirchweye. Both companies rounded up whatever German equipment they could find and put to use, and frequently came under enemy fire while so doing. Even without that harassment it was no mean task recovering damaged railway equipment on that sector. There was no bridge across the Rhine in the British sector, and the heavy breakdown equipment had to be worked from Nijmegen, through the American sector on a circuitous route to Rheine. However, by mid-April enough rolling stock had been collected around Osnabrück to enable No. 1 Operating Company to run 18 return trains per day between Rheine and Kirchweye. At first military signalling systems were in use as the German system had been considerably damaged.

The end of the war came before the Canadian Railway Group could make 'adequate and satisfactory preparations . . . A long-planned celebration had to be abandoned because of the "lack of spirits in this area which is absolutely dry"'. Any such celebrations would in any case have been short-lived for the Canadian railwaymen now faced the problems involved in carrying thousands of refugees to the west. Some crews were on turns of duty which lasted 72 hours, and they were grateful to have the use of German condenser engines. These locomotives had been designed for long runs on the Russian front where there might well be long distances between coalyards and effective water-towers. They had large tenders, and the spent steam was condensed, thus recovering some of the water. This meant fewer delays to take on coal or water and saved considerable time.

By the end of May German staff were ready to resume railway operations, and a progressive hand-over began. No. 1 Operating Company ceased to operate as a unit on 30th June, 1945, and No. 2 Operating Company was disbanded on 18th July. No. 1 Company was, however, recalled to action in late July in order to take over seven miles of track across the Belgian border into Aachen. To no-one's particular surprise, the Belgian and German railway staffs 'did not seem to be co-operating very well.' Consequently, No. 1 Company continued to operate the line until 13th October, and was then disbanded on 15th October.

No. 1 Railway Workshop Company had carried on wagon-building at Bruges, reaching a peak of 1,002 wagons in June 1945. A total of 6,000 wagons had been assembled by the time that the workshops were handed over to the 206th Railway Workshop Company, Royal Engineers. The Company HQ had moved to Knocke-sur-Mere prior to the hand-over, and the men were able 'to enjoy the seaside in off-duty hours for two summer months, before the unit was disbanded at Knocke on 24th September, 1945.'

Only the Headquarters Company then remained. 'Finally, the last 10 men on strength left Rheine on 29th November, driving six stores-laden vehicles to the dump at Nijmegen. Later that day the Canadian railway troops of the Second World War "became a memory"'.

A bright spot in the day! The mailman Private Hanson hands out the post for Company A.   *Authors' Collection*

Chapter Six
'Over There'
(Royal Engineers' Railwaymen Overseas)

To American railroad men service on the military railways at Longmoor and Melbourne was 'Over there', far from home, as indeed it was to Canadians, Australians, New Zealanders and men from the Empire. To people in Britain 'Over there' meant service in Europe or in one of the many theatres of war defending the Empire overseas. This chapter outlines some activities of Royal Engineers overseas.

Just before the outbreak of war in 1939 an Anglo-French agreement was concluded that the British Army would build all new rail facilities required by the intended operations of the British Expeditionary Force. To this end the following units accompanied the BEF to France at the start of its operations:

29th Railway Survey Company
150th ⎫
151st ⎬
152nd ⎭
8th Railway Construction and Operating Company.

Early on in 1940 four more railway construction companies joined their comrades in France, but the work of railway construction was limited to developing new rail-served depots and building new feeder lines to airfields. Nevertheless, by April 1940, 141 miles of track had been laid and 100 shunting locomotives had been shipped out from England and were operating in France. RE crews worked main line trains between St Malo and Rennes as well as carrying on their more usual activity of running trains in depots.

However, the late Spring of 1940 saw the German offensive in the west which, for many allied forces, ended at the beaches of Dunkirk or the French channel ports. Like many other units, Royal Engineers arrived back in England without most of their equipment, although one group did manage to bring the Brown hoist mentioned earlier. Perhaps the story of Sapper Eric Horsnall is typical of the many told of the retreat from France.

Eric's mother received a letter from him assuring her that all was well. That same morning she was in the village shop when a friend mentioned that he had seen Eric a short time earlier 'on the back of a motor bike'. Mrs Horsnall denied the possibility of this and referred to the letter just received from France. She was, therefore, not a little surprised to find a tired but happy son waiting at home when she returned from her shopping. He had almost caught up with his letter written several days earlier, and had arrived in Britain without even his boots; but he lived to fight another day. So began what was to be the long drag back to D-Day, but before the invasion of Europe, REs were active in many other theatres of war.

During the pursuit of the Axis forces from El Alamein to Tunis – October 1941 to May 1943 – a pause occurred while a forward base was established at Benghazi and forward troops probed a strong enemy position at El Agheila. Advantage of this was taken to improve communications, and rail communications in particular. Railway Construction Companies worked round the clock to ensure the opening of a railhead at Capuzzo by 21st November, 1942 and at Tobruk by 1st December. The final success of the British 8th and 1st Armies in North Africa depended greatly on the maintenance of these lines of communication.

George Williams went out to the Middle East in March 1941. His first attempt was in January 1941, but he got no further than Greenock as the ship on which he was embarked – the *Louis Pasteur* – was sabotaged by its French-Canadian crew. On arriving in Palestine a month or two later, he went to Haifa to join No. 199 Railway Workshop. Subsequently he was moved to Rafah near Ghaza in the Sinai Desert where British and Australian engineers built a large ordnance depot with some 22 miles of sidings. The rolling stock at the time consisted of three small tank engines – possibly Hunslet's – one of which, to George's delight, was fitted with Walschaert's valve gear with a slide valve rather then a piston valve. George had little experience of this and he looked upon his discovery as a valuable opportunity to learn.

After about a year George joined the newly-formed No. 182 Railway Operating Company under Major Bob Franklyn. This Company worked the line from Kantara to El Arish and Ghaza, with some trains worked through to Lydda. The locomotives in use at first were American Baldwin 4–6–0s, but later a number of old Robinson 2–8–0s were sent out, in poor condition. Many were without water-gauge protectors.

> We used to run around with perhaps one protector on, and hope for the best with the others. What's more, all we had in the cab was a hurricane lamp. That's all the light we had. Obviously, we didn't have any lights on the front or anything else, and they were very hot engines to work on. They'd only got a small cab, and the coal we had – I'd no idea where it came from, but I had a suspicion it came from Kenya; I might be wrong on that – it was very dirty coal, and after running 75 miles we had to clean out the fire. It'd take two of us, with shirts off, an hour to get it out. It'd be up to the firehole. All you had on top was a layer of fire, the rest was ashes or clinker. From a pulling point of view we found them very good engines, and a good engine to fire, and they did some sterling work. It was just the coal that was the problem. After they'd been there for a little while, there was some decision made at some level, and 199 Workshops, who were in Haifa, converted some from coal-burning to coal-and-oil-burning. It wasn't much of a conversion, and it wasn't a costly job. All they did, if I remember rightly, was to put some bricks in the firebox, and broken bricks on the bars; then just inside the firehole door we had a little coal fire, and in the firehole was fitted the nozzle of the oil burner. The thing was that you kept the fire going just to light the nozzle. From a steaming point of view, generally they weren't much good, but they gave me one and I had it quite a lot of trips. Eventually, I fiddled about with the burner and I got it to steam very well indeed.

Some of the Baldwins were similarly converted, and George recalls an incident with one of these converted locomotives – No. 913. The block post ('You couldn't call it a station') consisted of the main line, a loop line and a siding line. One night George, with No. 913, was crossing a train into the siding when the points were half-cocked. George could not see this as it was dark. 'The next thing I knew; the whole thing was off the rails, bouncing in the sand. The tender was in danger of toppling over and fouling the main line so it was shored up with old sleepers. It was later put back on the rails by a crane, and towed back to Kantara and put back into steam.' There seems doubt about the extent of the examination of the boiler because on the next trip the firebox crown-plate collapsed, and the driver died from the scalds he had received.

Royal Engineers who had been used to working with the old LNER 2–8–0s and the 'RODs' were amazed to receive some American 2–8–2 locos, and, says George Williams, 'Of course I'd never seen such luxury in a locomotive in all my life. We actually had seats to sit on, proper seats; and there were two or three little gauge lamps. It was like sitting in the cockpit of an aeroplane . . . all the gauges there!'

These particular locomotives were coal burners and well liked by the British crews. The 'front end' – cylinders and valves – was excellent, and their only weakness was the poor tyres on the coupled wheels. Later they received the same type of locomotive as a pure oil burner. Lack of familiarity with this type of engine might explain one dramatic incident.

The driver had left the engine in the care of the fireman when they stopped for water. The fireman turned on the oil flow, but did not turn on the steam to blow it up the firebox to ignite it from the heat of the box. The oil flowed and filled the ashpan until eventually it exploded. The heat was such that the locomotive was welded to the rails. The axle-boxes had seized and the springs were hanging like strings. This was the engine's first trip out, and when they did manage to move her she was abandoned in a siding.

George Williams tells an amusing story of his own first experience with one of these oil burners:

Now, the only experience we'd had was with a coal-oil-burner where you had a little coal fire which ignited the oil. You got steam up with the coal, then went over to oil, but with these new things you got steam up from another source, as we found out eventually; but this was the first one for us. There was a different arrangement in the firebox – it was more solid and it had air vents, obviously – so they actually got steam up by burning some old sleepers. When we got down to the shed at Kantara this thing had got steam up to about 100 lb, and nobody had bothered about the oil-burner . . . leave that to somebody else, you know! Nobody had any instructions, so my fireman looked at me and said, 'What are we going to do?' He was a bit of a droll Manchester lad, and I said, 'Well, Cliff, I'm not quite sure.' So, we had a look round this thing, and we decided we'd turn all the valves we could see, (except the main oil supply valve which he controlled) halfway. We thought, well, we can't go wrong with everything turned on halfway. Anyway, we lit it up and it started to go; the oil flow was coming and everything was burning nicely, thank you. We threw some waste into the firebox, then after a while the oil stopped flowing and all we got was a jet of steam coming through and nothing happening. Suddenly, 'WHOOSH', and there were fire and flames and smoke coming out of the chimney. Of course, we didn't know any better and we thought, well, perhaps it does this naturally. Anyway, off we went, and that was how we carried on: the fire went out, the steam went back, then 'WHOOSH' flames came out of the chimney top and you thought everything was going to explode.

We went on like this for about 50 miles, until I said to Cliff, 'You know I'm sure there's something we're not doing right. Let's have another look round.' So, we stopped and had another look at everything. We'd opened this valve quite innocently, not knowing quite what we were doing, and on the side of the firebox was a little cylinder – it was part of the fuel line to the burner – which the pipe went through. Now, what actually happened was . . . when we opened one valve we actually allowed steam into this cylinder which built up a pressure over the course of time and stopped the oil flowing. The object of this steam pipe and the valve going into this cylinder and into the main oil supply was: when you closed down the engine you opened this valve to clear the fuel line. Great excitement on our part . . . but when we got it going, it really went!

Diesel locomotives were beginning to make their appearance during this time. At Rafah, for instance, there were US Gardner 0–6–0 shunting engines which worked as well as their compressed air starters would allow, and on the Kantara – Lydda line were diesel-electrics. They were 650 hp, powered by two caterpillar tractor engines, the cab being in the middle with an engine and generator at each end, and two four-wheeled bogies. When being used in tandem a driver was needed for each locomotive as they lacked facilities for dual control, but for their purpose they were very efficient.

Aid to our Russian ally depended on effective maintenance of difficult lines of communication. The daunting task of the Royal Navy and of the Merchant Navy in trying to supply an ungrateful ally by sea has been well described – though no-one who did not take part can probably appreciate the full horrors of the Arctic convoys. Railway engineers, however, also played their part in the task of supplying the USSR.

In October 1941 an engineering force was sent to Persia (Iran) to increase the capacity of the line from the Persian Gulf to the Caspian Sea from 200 tons per day to over 2,000 tons per day. The line started at a deep water jetty on the Persian Gulf and ran at first through flat country. An engineer officer describes the rest of the line:

> For the next hundred or so miles the railway wound through deep gorges, over numerous bridges, and through a hundred long and often spiral tunnels, climbing steadily . . . to 7,000 feet. From Teheran the railway traversed another 300 miles of heavy country crossing the Alburz Mountains by 2.3 per cent grades with magnificently aligned and engineered tunnels, spirals and bridges which make this part of the line comparable with some of the mighty railway achievements in the Rockies in Canada and the USA . . . The railway had been well-engineered and built, but was a single line equipped only for a few light trains . . . Our target was 2,400 tons per day of useful 'Aid to Russia' traffic and we aimed at 12 to 15 trains per day.

The initial development was undertaken by Indian Engineers and units from Britain arrived in February 1942. In June 1942 the first US Engineers arrived, and the whole line was taken over by them by April 1943. At that time most of the physical reconstruction had been completed, and a sound organisation had been established for traffic control and maintenance. In the hands of the US Engineers the capacity of the line was further developed and reached a daily peak of 10,000 tons of war material to Russia. Between October 1941 and October 1944 over four million tons of war supplies had been delivered to Russia by rail.

This was a considerable contribution to the allied war effort by railway engineers from three continents. Whilst not comparing with the perils of the

Arctic convoys, it represents a magnificent feat by the Construction Companies and extreme devotion to duty by the Operating Companies. Taking a heavily-laden steam train through difficult terrain was exhausting work, and crews often emerged from long, spiralling tunnels hardly able to draw breath let alone feed the fire or control the locomotives.

Eventually the focus of attention shifted back to Europe, and in September 1943 the Allies invaded Italy. In the same month 160th Railway Construction Company were given responsibility for re-opening the east coast railway from Taranto. Three important bridges on this line were replaced with Bailey Bridges. As mentioned in Chapter Four, Bailey equipment was not normally suitable for railway work, but piers were erected with trestling and proved quite serviceable. 586 Field Company erected one using three spans of 40 ft, 80 ft and 40 ft; the second was erected by 587 Field Company with three spans of 60 ft and the third consisted of a single 40 ft span erected by 561 Field Company.

In mid-October 1943, while developing the east coast railway, 160th Company was joined by 10th Railway Company, and in the west 161st Railway Company took responsibility for the development of the Naples – Salerno line. After a re-allocation of duties between American and British units, 150th Railway Construction Company undertook the repair of the Caserta–Foggia line, and 161st worked out from Naples to Caserta to join up with them, assisted by the 1st Bridging Section of 167th Company. Operation of the line was taken over by the Italian State Railways as soon as such operation became practicable as the lines advanced.

Mussolini had been overthrown in July 1943, and his successor, Marshal Badoglio, concluded an armistice with the Allies in September. Any hopes that the Allied leaders might have had of an easy advance through Italy were soon dashed by German Forces determined not to give up so easily, and the Italian campaign soon fell into stalemate. In January 1944 landings at Anzio, designed to break the deadlock, met little success, and memories of Gallipoli were revived. It was not until 4th June, 1944 that Rome fell, by which time the thoughts of the highest commanders were elsewhere in Europe.

British and allied armies were about to return to the beaches of France, and engineers of all specialisms had significant roles in the latest act of the great drama of these years. Clearly, Sappers would be needed early on the beaches to deal with anti-tank placements, mines and suchlike, but the railway engineers were not far behind the initial invasion. Indeed, an officer of the Bridging School, 1st Lieutenant Alan Becket made an important contribution to Operation Overlord in designing the kite anchor for use with Mulberry Harbours.

Following the consolidation of the initial bridgehead in Normandy the town of Caen was the immediate objective of the British forces under Montgomery. It proved to be a hard nut to crack, and was subjected to heavy bombing by RAF and USAAF, before the invading forces could move in; ironically, the severe bomb damage at Caen made progress through the town extremely difficult and slow for the advancing forces. Some impression of the damage at Caen can be gained from the photograph on the next page.

As soon as the enemy was cleared from Caen work started to restore it as a main centre for railway traffic. The Official History records that workshops and railway installations were completely destroyed, mainly by allied bombing, but locomotive repairs began on 14th August, 1944, and work was begun to clear a route to the Seine.

Ted Baller went to France on about D-Day plus ten with No. 3 Railway Operating Group, and was outside Caen for some time waiting to help restore rail communications. They were billeted in a small village called Callarmes consisting of only about a dozen houses. The private house to which Ted was assigned was normally occupied by a single woman, but it now accommodated nine men too. The owner was allocated one room upstairs and one downstairs, a second upstairs room being occupied by a French captain who acted as an interpreter. The other eight soldiers occupied the remaining upstairs room. Bathtime was interesting: water had to be boiled in two gallon jerricans, and baths had to be taken after dark to avoid giving smoke-signals. Ted Baller reminisces: 'When we finally got into Caen it was terrible. There was no water. You had to go out of Caen for water with a tank on the back of a Jeep, and you put Chloros in the water. Oh, it was horrible.' The troops sorted out the yards as quickly as possible in order to get American supply trains through. Not that their own supplies always reached them on time, but natural resourcefulness saw them through: 'If you were short of grub you used to stop the American trains, burst a lock off a wagon and get boxes of food out. You had to keep surviving.'

Ken Hicklin and Sam Ernill were with 197 Company at Caen where they built the first replacement railway bridge and then moved on to Bayeux. Supplies were still coming through the Mulberry Harbour, but wherever possible, local materials were used. When they reached Bayeux they stopped importing sleepers and used green timber cut down locally by a Canadian Forestry Company. Like the railway companies, the forestry companies worked 8 hr shifts around the clock, and the work was hard. This did not deter the Foresters from making regular calls on 'girl-friends' in the village before returning to their billets. Neither of their energetic pursuits seemed to dim their enthusiasm for the other.

The railway bridge over the Rue de la Gore, Caen viewed from the north side on 23rd July, 1944.
Authors' Collection

A considerable amount of material was stored at Bayeux, and 197 Company had 50 to 60 lorries lined up on the roadway – mainly three-tonners, but later they did acquire some American low-loaders. In the confusion of war it would have been surprising if nothing had gone wrong, and mistakes were indeed made. Fortunately these were rare and none too serious, but occasionally they had their comic aspect. Some marker-buoys had been ordered for a river crossing, and they duly arrived – each eight feet high and needing a 3 ton lorry to carry it. Sea-buoys had been sent instead of those for marking river channels.

It was in the advance in Europe that Lt Colonel Everall's Unit Construction Railway Bridge made its greatest contribution to the war, and 197 Company was responsible for a spectacular bridging operation across the Seine at Le Manoir. As the Official History records, there was very heavy damage to all rail installations, and eventually the site at Le Manoir was selected for the crossing. The bridge was to be 520 ft long and subsequently necessitated the removal of 90,000 cubic yards of earth for the approach works. After only 14 days the bridge was opened to traffic on 22nd September, 1944. Until the Channel ports north of the Seine were opened to traffic, this bridge was, for two months, the main line of maintenance for forces operating to the north. For example, it provided the only guaranteed supply line for fuel for the advance armour units. There was an anxious period when the River Seine suffered its worst flood for 40 years, and the bridge was inundated almost to rail-level, but it held and trains continued to pass over it throughout the flood. The Official History of the Royal Canadian Engineers includes the following account of the worst period of danger to the bridge:

> The major worry at the time was the Le Manoir railway bridge near Pont de l'Arche, a temporary army structure which was only just surviving the very high and repeated floods of the Seine. Towards the end of November, in the dark hours of a rainy morning, 22 cars of coal had to be rushed to the crossing from Louviers to weight the super-structure down. The deck was later jacked up to clear the flood, but the bridge was by no means out of danger. On 5th December, when the tracks were beginning to look like a miniature roller-coaster, with water up to the base of the line, engines were taken off the bridge. Trains were coupled up and pushed across in a continuous string of cars to be uncoupled and receive a new engine on the far side – an inconvenient but safer system for the crews . . .
>
> . . . on 6th February it again became necessary to weight the Le Manoir bridge with loaded cars. Surprisingly, the structure held together and survived the winter.

Lt Colonel Everall might have been less surprised. The story of this bridge is told graphically in the accompanying photographs.

When Calais was liberated it quickly became a centre for transhipment of equipment to the advancing allied forces. Ted Baller went to Calais, but his immediate concerns were not with railway equipment, but with the well-being of his men. 'The first thing I did was to close the brothel.'

Having sorted that out other matters could be attended to and the Company was responsible for loading and unloading cross-channel boats, mainly

The original Seine bridge at Le Manoir consisted of three lattice spans supported on two masonry piers. Owing to its complete demolition (*seen above*) a new low level bridge was constructed being of 534 ft span consisting of two 40 ft approach and six 75 ft deck type URCB spans carried on seven piers.   *Authors' Collection*

The above shows the new approach on the east side, the placing of one of the wet piers and the building of UCRB spans on the approach line.   *Authors' Collection*

This view shows three UCRB spans in position and the launching of the remaining three UCRB spans.   *Authors' Collection*

The finished bridge under its first test with apprehensive eyes watching from the shore and the river. The work was commenced on 4th September, 1944 and finished on 22nd September, 1944. For passage of river traffic, one of the spans was at a later date converted to a through type lifting span.   *Authors' Collection*

The finished bridge alongside the wrecked original. During November and December the worst floods for 34 years for the time of the year were experienced and the water level rose to the rail level, but the bridge weathered the conditions and traffic continued to pass with little delay.   *Authors' Collection*

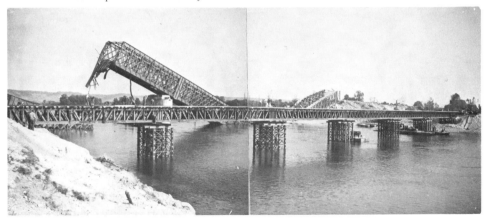

The approach to the 'new' bridge at Le Manoir. A driver's view from aboard the first train.   *Authors' Collection*

of American locomotives and RAF long-loaders. A boat had to be unloaded and re-loaded in about 50 minutes to turn round on the tide, so speed was essential. Sometimes men had their own reasons for haste. Ted Baller recalls, 'This shunter from Cardiff, he had a date . . . and he took a lot of risks. He got one of these American engines off the line, and he said, "If Ted comes down here there won't half be a row" so he got some fishplates under the wheel and got it back on.'

As the fighting front advanced railway engineers moved on into Belgium and Holland. After his return from the Middle East George Williams spent some time in Derby, and later at Eastleigh, before going to Holland shortly before Christmas in 1944. Railway operating there was dangerous work for the railways were subject to constant air attack. George was attacked by enemy aircraft on two occasions, the most frightening incident being on New Year's morning 1945. He relates,

> There'd been several attacks, and trains were burning all around, and this figher plane came at us and we stopped. I put the brake on and my fireman and I, we were down the embankment as fast as we could. It was a lovely moonlight morning; just a sprinkle of snow on the ground, and we went down this embankment and into a

field out of the way a bit. Let 'im have a go at it if he wanted. We stayed there while the pilot made several strafing runs. Then the loco. began blowing off steam, so we decided that somebody had to go back, and it had to be me because I was the driver. Now, when we came down the embankment there was some barbed wire, but we got through with no trouble. Getting back was a different story, but I managed to get back on the engine and put some more water in the boiler, and lie down out of the way. Eventually, the pilot had to go; I suppose he'd used up all his ammo.

George and his fireman were lucky. A cannon shell had passed through the front part of the cab, and would surely have killed one of them if they had stayed on the footplate.

From Eindhoven George's unit moved to 's-Hertogenbosch on the line to Utrecht where George acted as running foreman. A good many train crews were lost in this area from aerial attack as there were regular raids on the trains. George says, 'They used to shoot right into the cab, you know. They really had a bang at us.'

As related in Chapter Two, Longmoor-trained men opened up the line to Nijmegen and later, George worked the line between Nijmegen and Cleves, a distance of about 26 miles. Here they operated with Riddles-designed 'Austerity' 2−8−0s which were clearly disliked by the crews: 'At over 30 miles an hour you could neither sit, stand nor lie on the damn things.'

George drove Leave-trains on the line between Gott and Krefeld, and also Krefeld to Tilburg. At Krefeld was an electrically-operated turntable, and the German locomotives, although battered, were a revelation to any British railwayman. They had comfortable cabs, electric lighting and cab lighting, dropping grates and rocking bars. George commented, 'When they saw the "Austerities" they just shook their heads, and I think they wondered how we'd won the war. They saw me flapping about with an old paraffin lamp oiling up, and a paraffin lamp on the front, and a paraffin lamp to light up the gauge column – that's all we had – they just shook their heads; and when we started shovelling the clinker out with a shovel, that was the end as far as they were concerned.'

A German engine driver at Krefeld reckoned that they had lost about 80 per cent of their footplate staff, killed or wounded. George Williams had great admiration for the German railwaymen and he tells of how their ingenuity kept trains running at a junction where points and signals had been destroyed. They managed to get the points working, then placed a searchlight on the remains of the signal box. This light was played on to the locomotive and then swung in the required direction of travel.

The Rhine was bridged at Spyck. As there was no previous rail crossing there, approach lines had to be built. The estimated time for doing the job was two-and-a-half months, but it was done in one month. The bridge was 2,368 ft long and opened just in time for the end of the war. The end of the war, however, meant more work for the military engineers. First, they had to clear damaged installations, and Royal Engineers built 500 bridges and opened 6,000 miles of railway in Germany in 1945−46. Over the first three months of Peace traffic was increased from 13,000 tons per day to 150,000 tons per day: a tremendous tribute to their training and skill.

Chapter Seven

'It's Foolish but it's Fun'
(The Lighter Side of Service Life)

Despite the privations of life in a wartime army, many of which are well remembered, the abiding memories of life at Longmoor and Melbourne are ones of cheerfulness and, sometimes, hilarity. We have met or corresponded with no-one who does not have affectionate recollections of one or the other, or even both. All remember the comradeship of those years and the many, many humorous incidents which punctuated their daily routine.

One such incident occurred after a member of the MT Section at Longmoor took up angling in a nearby lake. Having had no luck whatsoever, he and a mate determined that their next visit would be more successful. It was. With a few railway detonators they blasted to the surface more fish than they could possibly deal with, leaving a fair number of dead fish floating on the surface of the lake, and many puzzled villagers wondering what had caused the condition.

A similar occurrence happened at Melbourne though the circumstances were different. There, for reasons never divulged, a young lieutenant ordered his men to throw detonators into a lake in the grounds of a mansion just outside the small town. The subsequent explosion brought shoals of dead fish to the surface, and the officer was at a loss as to what to do with them. Eventually he ordered the troops to use their 'tin helmets' to scoop out as many fish as possible, and then to use the same helmets as spades to dig holes in the ground and bury the fish!

The 'Flying Bull' at Rake was a favourite rendezvous for off-duty REs, from Longmoor. One night, after drinking there until 23.00 hours, six members of the MT section took an ambulance for an unofficial trip. Sleeping residents of the barrack block were awakened by the noisy arrival of the ambulance. When they looked out they saw a body being carried on a stretcher from the vehicle. 'Poor old Bert,' they wondered. 'What's happened to him?' They crowded round the supine figure wrapped in blankets. Bert opened his eyes, and struggled to speak – a message for anxious relatives? Yes – he managed to gasp, 'I'm as p..... as a newt!' and lapsed unconscious again.

Sergeant Nash and Corporal Cloake took to an unusual means of transport when leaving the 'Flying Bull'. No motor vehicle being available, they commandeered a tandem and set off along the country lanes. The effects of the ale and their unfamiliarity with the machine combined, as they sped down a steep hill, to ensure that they did not negotiate the bend at the bottom. They finished up in a watercress bed, much more sober and very wet.

A good rapport between officers and men is essential in any fighting unit, and we have heard many stories which testify to this spirit at the Railway Training Centres.

Members of the MT Section meeting newly-commissioned officers at Longmoor, for example, adopted the trick of saluting, doubling back round the workshop, then saluting again. So pleased were they to receive their first salutes that the officers rarely recognised the 'second' lot as the people who had saluted only minutes before. Then there is the tale of the two sappers from Longmoor who were posted to Alton where the Headquarters was housed in a requisitioned mansion. Marching up the drive, they met an officer cycling down, and saluted him smartly. The rider removed his left hand from the handlebars to tuck his cane under his left arm, at the same time as he attempted to salute with his right. The result was predictable and one red-faced officer was soon picking himself and his bicycle off the ground. Our informant did not record what assistance he was given by the two men.

Relations at Melbourne were less formal. A certain Captain was notorious for his attention to detail and his habit of making spot checks at any time. Ken Smethurst went on to relate how a Lance-Corporal became so annoyed with the Captain following him around that he suddenly stopped, turned round and told him to clear off. The Captain apologised and did as he was commanded.

Sometimes humour had its darker side, as the treatment of one lad stationed at Weston Camp typifies. One day the air-raid sirens sounded, and he dived straight into a hut out of the way. His mates, rather disgusted, threw ashes on to the corrugated iron roof so that it sounded like falling shrapnel. The occupant came out, trembling. Every time he went into the hut the action was repeated as a reminder of the occasion, but if he was ever near the hut when the sirens wailed, he always went in it.

Melbourne is a well-known market-gardening area, and men stationed in the area would often find beautiful, large mushrooms in the fields. One soldier came back with some which were shared around through breakfast. When they were all eating heartily, one man winked at his mates and began to hold his stomach and groan. All the other chaps, except the mushroom-picker, picked up the trick and started moaning and groaning. Quite soon the mushroom-gatherer became convinced that he had eaten toadstools, and to the amusement of everyone else he was made physically sick just by the suggestion from his mates.

Natural history seems to have interested the men at Longmoor, too. George Grouch and Bernard Cloake were out testing a 3 ton lorry one day when they passed a forest where they saw plants which looked like giant rhubarb: the stems were about three inches or more thick with a leaf span of about seven feet. They stopped and cut some for a bit of fun back at camp, when a Forestry Commission ranger approached. A couple of weeks' 'Jankers' seemed inevitable as he asked what they were doing. 'We're taking this back to camp for botany classes,' said Bernard Cloake.

'Oh, that's all right then,' said the ranger. Relieved, they took their prize back to camp, and left it in a place of honour in the office of Second Lieutenant Pat Ford, where it remained a source of amusement for some time afterwards.

The church at Breedon-On-The-Hill is a dominant feature of the landscape around Melbourne, and at the height of the invasion scare in 1940 Royal Engineers from Melbourne were allotted guard duties on the hill top. A duty squad consisted of nine men: two on the hill and the rest in 'The Hollybush

Inn' at Breedon with a connecting field telephone. Of the two on the hill top, one patrolled and one manned the telephone, calling the 'Hollybush' every half-hour to report in. If no 'phone call came and the guard could not be raised, then the squad set off up the hill to investigate. One bright, sunny day there was no reply from the hill top so the Sergeant-Major went to investigate. He found that the duty guard was lying on a bank, talking to some girls, his rifle being laid aside. The Sergeant-Major was able to pick up the rifle and walk away with it unseen. This dereliction of duty resulted in 28 days' field punishment for the culprit, after which he was never the same again.

Breedon Church was also the setting of another incident – either funny or grim, according to how you look at it. One Sunday morning a zealous patrol was stopping all the cars as people went to church. One driver failed to stop when signalled so to do, so one of the patrol fired at the car, fortunately missing it. In the words of Ken Smethurst, 'The driver lost all the rubber on his tyres, stopped and staggered out of the car and sat down on the running board, frightened to death, trembling.'

Melbourne Church, on the other hand, held happier memories. On Ken Smethurst's first Sunday there, he recalled, only one lad went to church – to the amusement of everyone else. When he returned, however, he had the laugh on his mates for he had been invited to lunch with a local family on the following Sunday. Needless to say, the next Sunday saw the church full, and the vicar introduced each soldier to a family who invited most of the troops to lunch. As Ken said, 'It was worthwhile, and everybody went to church after that.'

Kit was often a problem – getting everything the right size and keeping it was an art in itself. One lad who had been posted to Bordon received what looked like a greatcoat of 1914 vintage. He went to a pub with his mates, hung up his coat and picked up another on the way out. It was no good – too small. It was not until his sixth attempt that he acquired a suitable coat together with 'no end of sweets and other different things in the pockets. But that was the game, really . . . If you lost anything in the Army, you pinched a replacement off somebody else!'

Syd Arkell who was yard-foreman at King's Newton from mid-1943 remembers a certain RE driver; a Cockney with a reputation for eccentric driving. On one occasion he was shunting some wagons at Worthington with a Midland 0–6–0 tank. Called back slowly, he came much too fast, braked hard but too late, and the wagons ended up in a pile at the bottom of the incline. Quite a number of firemen refused to work with this driver, and Syd hated to be on the same shift as he because there was always trouble. The line was controlled by tablet working, but the driver in question often ignored the tablets. His philosophy was simple: 'Oh, b..... the tablet – come on! If we hit something, we hit something.'

A certain character remembered from Longmoor, but who shall remain nameless, was a 'Salesman' that is a Royal Engineer who had a 'moonlight' job. He would go to local markets with a suitcase full of coloured candles cut into half-inch sections. At the market he would buy two pieces of meat or fish, drench one piece in eau-de-cologne and light a coloured candle by the side of it. The untreated piece was soon covered with flies; the other piece remained free of them. He sold the bits of candle for one shilling (5p) each. He also sold a liniment rub for backache. This concoction was made by rubbing a red 'donkey-stone' into a bath of water. The resulting red liquid was bottled and sold for half-a-crown a bottle (12½p). Not only did he sell it, but he had satisfied customers returning for more!

Probably the best remembered character at Longmoor was CSM Dimmock, described by George Grouch as 'a regular old soldier'. George affirms, 'He was a real terror. His voice used to terrorise new recruits, believe me.' One day George Grouch was on guard duty with 'Old guard' and 'New guard' facing each other for inspection. There came an almighty yell from Dimmock, foaming at the mouth and screaming at one of the guard. Some words could be made out, like, 'YOU! What do you think this is? A ...... fashion parade?' What crime had been committed? One of the guard was wearing his steel helmet at an angle.

Another 'Parade ground' story also concerned George Grouch. He and Bernard Cloake had the job of diagnosing and rectifying brake trouble on a Morris 15 cwt. truck. Having found the fault, they reckoned that they needed another half-hour to put the brakes right. At that moment in came the Duty Corporal: Corporal Shaw, well known for his short temper. He was shouting and rampaging because the job was not finished, and insisted on taking the truck for a test run. The MT workshops were close by the parade ground, and the impatient corporal found that he was unable to stop. He finished up in the centre of the sacred parade ground. He had great difficulty in explaining his act of sacrilege to a far from pleased senior officer.

There must be countless more anecdotes redolent of the humour of Service life in wartime. In the years from 1939 to 1945 men and women in uniform faced up to an existence that often placed them in great danger, and equally often confronted them with occurrences flavoured with the essence of great hilarity. In this book we hope that we have illustrated those facets of life in one of the Armed Services that did so much to assist in defeating an evil and pernicious political doctrine that threatened the world.

An LMS class '1F' 0–6–0 No. 1890 seen here at Melbourne on 25th October, 1943.
R.C. Riley

LMS locomotive class '1F' 0–6–0 No. 1839 waiting at King's Newton in 1943.
R.C. Riley Collection

Vulcan diesel hydraulic No. 4564, one of the first diesel Hydraulics to be operated in the United Kingdom seen at Melbourne in October 1943. *R.C. Riley Collection*

Appendix One

The Melbourne Military Railway – Signalling, Traffic and Motive Power

The portion of the Derby to Ashby branch-line taken over by the War Department in late 1939 lay between Chellaston East Junction and Smisby Road Bridge No. 43 just outside Ashby-de-la-Zouch. At this point a sleeper was placed across the metals to indicate the limit of military occupation. Military 'block posts' were established at Chellaston Quarry – eventually developed to succeed Melbourne as HQ of the line – where the operational control centre was set up; at King's Newton which gradually became a vast Transportation Stores and a training centre for port operators, handling staff and Railway Construction Companies; at Tonge and Breedon which served as the Castle Donington Vehicle Stores; at Newbold where there was an exit from New Lount Colliery; at Heath End, Ticknall where a military weighbridge was built, and at Smisby Road.

While preliminary work had been going on the national press wrongly reported that a line in the Midlands had been taken over by the War Department and was being fitted up with French signalling. However, the signalling system was as follows:

(a) *Chellaston Junction* (the box controlling the connection between the Stenson Junction line and the Derby line via Chellaston station) to *Chellaston Quarry* (1,600 yards): Double line block over LMS metals.

(b) *Chellaston Quarry to King's Newton*: (1 mile 100 yards level). Double line block with LMS block instruments. Military flagboards were set up at King's Newton, home and distant semaphores being replaced by metal plates painted green on one side and red on the reverse, one green board only representing a distant 'check'. The boards were replaced by handlamps at night.

(c) *King's Newton to Melbourne*: (540 yards level). Double line block with LMS instruments. Semaphore signals were controlled by Melbourne (Midland built) box. There was no distant for up trains – towards Ashby – but a distant fixed at Caution for down trains, at which one well-known character stood and whistled until otherwise persuaded by the blockman.

(d) *Melbourne to Tonge & Breedon*: (1 mile 1,348 yards on a slightly rising gradient). Single line military telephone and ticket at Tonge, with flagboards for up and down directions, plus an Annett's Key for each of the two ground frames. There was also an intermediate public siding at Wilson Bridge which served the village there and was worked by Annett's Key.

(e) *Tonge & Breedon to Worthington*: (1 mile, 1,685 yards on rising gradient 1 in 300 to 180). Electric miniature – Webb & Thompson. Full semaphore signalling for both directions.

(f) *Worthington to Newbold*: (1 mile, 485 yards on rising gradient 1 in 60). Tyers Electric Tablet.

(g) *Newbold to Heath End*: (1 mile, 661 yards rising 1 in 60 to 1 in 180). One engine in steam with special Caution ticket – Army Form A3128.

(h) *Heath End to Ticknall*: (1 mile, 30 yards rising 1 in 60 to 1 in 300). Army Form A3128.

(j) *Ticknall to Smisby Road*: (1,733 yards level). On the Smisby Road side of Ticknall Wharf was the main engineering feature of the line: the 650 yard tunnel known variously as Ticknall Old Tunnel and Smisby Tunnel. This was a very damp, rickety structure through which only ex-Midland Railway '1F' 0–6–0 tank engines were allowed, the speed limit being 10 mph.

Civilian Involvement

Although the War Department took over the actual operation of the line, the LMSR did retain agents, clerks and checkers at Melbourne, Tonge, Worthington and New Lount Colliery to deal with accountancy and other civilian railway purposes. One well-known civilian was Mr Bollard, the New Lount Colliery Manager who was a tough and unshakeable man. New Lount, a modern, well-equipped colliery had all mod. cons., for its staff, and the canteen cooking was notable for its excellence, a fact which many train-crews could confirm as being infinitely more appetising than haver-sack rations.

The output of the colliery was enormous, and the Army could never work empties there quickly enough. Twelve trains of up to 30 wagons were scheduled for each day, but special workings were almost daily occurrences. Mr Bollard was always on the rampage at the Wagon Controller for empties which were No. 1 priority in the up direction.

Traffic Priorities

Traffic was worked in a very strict priority order under the supervision of Chellaston Quarry Control:

Up to Ashby
1. Empty wagons and pit-props in truck-loads to New Lount Empty Sidings.
2. Empty hoppers and wagons to Worthington for ironstone traffic.
3. Milk-van Melbourne – off the 06.00 ex-Chaddesden – and other perishables for LMS stations.
4. Out-crop coal wagons and other empty wagons as required. Out-crop coal was being worked near Newbold village and Heath End.

Down from Ashby
1. War Department Shipment traffic from Transportation Stores, King's Newton, including many out-of-gauge loads.
2. Perishable traffic, e.g. sugar beet from Ticknall Old Wharf, and farm produce ex-Melbourne.
3. Coal from New Lount Loaded sidings.
4. Stone and lime traffic ex-Worthington.
5. Out-crop coal picked up at Ticknall.
6. Other stations' traffic, e.g. WD transport such as Bren carriers, lorries, and various other forms of Army transport which had been repaired at Castle Donington and picked up at Tonge & Breedon; Home Guard ammunition from Worthington.

The traffic under (6) was at first worked down rough to Chellaston Quarry, so it is perhaps necessary to explain the layout of this main exchange point with the LMSR.

Links with the LMSR

At the beginning of 1940 there were three exchange sidings on the down side of the yard, with up and down 'main' lines between these and the up yard. The latter eventually consisted of 11 roads – one cripple siding – of 300 wagons' capacity.

Traffic for the LMS was picked up by that company's locomotives which worked in on the up main, either with a train, or Engine and Brake, or Light Engine. If it had a train, it would work forward and push it back into Quarry

Yard. If it had a brake van only, it would cross over at Quarry Blockpost – at the Ashby end of the yard – and back the brake on to the rear end of its train in the exchange sidings. The loco was then 'offered' to Chellaston Junction by Quarry Box, and ran round the exchange sidings to the Main Outer Home where it was admitted to the train in the exchange sidings by Annett's Key.

At a later stage in the development of the line, LMS locos worked trains to and from King's Newton, but many of the drivers had to take on a military pilot. In all there were 12 up and 12 down booked LMS workings, including block coal for Buildwas Power Station – via Chellaston Junction, Stenson Junction, Stoke and Crewe. Block stone for Wellingborough Corby was propelled to Chellaston Junction crossover and thence via Weston and Trent Junction. There were also many unprogrammed workings when traffic out of the MMR was heavy and extra trains were needed. Other booked workings were the Army's own 'four days a week' recreational trains to Derby, and daily work trains for Derby Works. These were worked by military enginemen and guards passed in LMS rules, regulations and road-knowledge by LMS Loco and Signalling Inspectors.

Yard Layouts

Details of the individual yards and premises, as at the beginning of 1943, are given here:

Chellaston Quarry

The line HQ was situated here together with a Control Office which housed a selective ringing telephone system covering the blockposts and offices along the line. There were clerical offices, and one for the Loco foreman who was in charge of the two-road shed which had inspection pits, storage sidings, a fire pit and a coaling stage. The water column was located at the point of convergence of the various shed roads, and was fed by a pump from the River Trent. This pump was coal-fired and worked by its own operator whose trade was designated as centrifugal pump attendant. One feature of the shed area was a coal-stack line at the end of which was housed an ex-LNWR saddle tank No. 27477 used for instructional purposes.

In the yard sidings were usually allocated to destinations, trains being marshalled as circumstances required. Controlling the yard was a five-lever ground frame with LMS block instruments working to Chellaston Junction and King's Newton. All shunting had to be carried out on the up main except for short rakes which could be accommodated by the spur. The limit of shunt was the Quarry up starter, the only signal worked from the box. A scissors crossover was situated at the throat of the yard, and military flag-boards were employed as signals on the down line. LMS trains working in were backed straight into the yard. Although, strictly speaking, no shunting was allowed with LMS locomotives, trains were usually broken up by them, as required.

On each shift staff included a yardmaster, three shunters – one for the exchange sidings – a checker and two wagon examiners.

King's Newton

This site was to become one of the largest Transportation Stores in the country. Early in 1943 it comprised only 12 double-ended tracks, but by the end of that year RE Construction Companies had so enlarged the depot that it was split into three sub-depots, each with 20–30 roads, some of which were a mile long. In addition six exchange sidings were laid to enable LMS trains to run through without calling at Quarry. The value of this became clear as D-Day preparations intensified, and block trains of Transportation material were working out of the MMR.

A combined blockpost and ground frame controlled the entrance to the depot. Ordinary LMS block instruments were used to Quarry and Melbourne, locking the starters at these boxes, but no semaphores were provided, flagboards being used.

Melbourne
The Midland-built box was manned by military blockmen. There was the usual range of country station traffic including a milk van which worked away to Chaddesden (Derby) at 07.40 hours each morning.

Wilson Bridge
This was merely a delivery siding for Wilson village.

Tonge & Breedon
The purely civilian traffic was similar to that of Melbourne. There was, however, an intensive military vehicle traffic connected with the RASC and RAOC depots at the pre-war Donington Park motor-racing circuit. The former passenger platform was still in situ, but there were extensive sidings. Ground frames controlled movements on to and off the main line at each end of the yard and, what with flag-boards as well, the blockman needed to be quite an athlete.

Worthington
An extremely busy iron and limestone quarry with daily block trains to Corby and Wellingborough. The station buildings were intact and there was a Midland-built signal box and water tower.

Newbold
Laid out here were the New Lount Colliery empty and loaded sidings, while on the west side of the main line were the sidings of the Leicester Pipe Company. The colliery sidings formed a triangle with the main line, but the military working stopped at propelling wagons into the empties sidings (which held 100 wagons and were often full) after knocking the brake off into the spur. The next move was forward, then reverse on to the brake which had been run out by the guard on to the main line. The loco now moved away to the loaded sidings, picked up the train, brought it out on to the mainline and backed it on to the brake. Daily loads included a block load for Buildwas – already mentioned earlier – but by the end of 1943 this train was run via Birmingham (Saltley and Bordesley GWR).

Heath End
This was used only for the training of brakesmen and shunters. Entry to the siding was by ground frame which was locked by the key issued at the same time as the Army Form A3128 – the Caution ticket.

Ticknall Old and New Wharfs
The Old Wharf was part of the original 1799 plateway, but it was expanded by the Royal Engineers. The Old Wharf handled sugar beet and local produce while the New Wharf handled out-crop coal, for which purpose the weighbridge was installed.

Ticknall to Bridge 43
At Smisby Road the Army laid three training sidings, and Bridge 43 was the nightly de-training point from a train of ex-North Eastern Railway clerestory-roofed coaches for a horde of Sappers who preferred the bright lights of Ashby-de-la-Zouch to the fleshpots of Derby.

A WD 0−6−0 diesel shunter, No. 26, at Melbourne. *R.C. Riley*

Armstrong Whitworth diesel shunter LMS No. 7062 taken on to the RE strength at Melbourne. *R.C. Riley*

Motive Power

The locomotive stock varied, but there were certain 'fixtures', notably six ex-Midland class '1F' 0–6–0 tank engines: Nos. 1666, 1710, 1788, 1839, 1889 and 1895 – all Westinghouse fitted, and four with open-backed cabs. Locomotive No. 1839 was a remarkable little engine which regularly did the 7 miles into Derby in 10 minutes flat, with 120 tons gross behind her. Many were the Derby enginemen who complained that the Army had taken their best tank loco. She survived military handling, and went to her rest from Derby depot in June 1956.

Other permanent allocations were two ex-LSWR Adams 0–4–2s, Nos. 614 and 618, both graceful engines with a fair turn of speed. These were also used on the Derby trains. No. 614 once distinguished – or disgraced – herself by dropping a plug with a full boiler across the up and down main lines in Chaddesden yard.

There were also LMS '4F' 0–6–0s Nos. 3836–9, for the coal trains, as well as an LMS Armstrong-Whitworth diesel No. 7062. Another diesel in stock was No. 4564 (its works number) which was one of the first diesel-hydraulics in this country. She had been built by Vulcan Foundry to an order from Vulkan of Germany. She was offered to the main line companies, but they declined the offer so the War Department took her on strength. Nobody at Chellaston was allowed to touch her except a Sgt Wilson and two Corporal drivers, simply because nobody else could understand the hydraulic transmission. Despite this cosseting, she was a frequent failure, and rarely worked beyond Melbourne. She was sent to UNRRA in November 1946.

Visitors included GWR Dean 0–6–0s Nos. WD 93 and 99 as well as a number of USA Transportation Corps locomotives – 0–6–0 tanks which were very powerful with a brake like the kick of a mule, and connecting rods suspected of being made from plastic because they were always bending. The SR bought some of them after the war for use in Southampton Docks, and two survive on private lines here.

The other main class to work on the MMR was the Austerity 0–6–0 tanks which were sturdy little locos that saw service on the Continent. Some stayed in France and Holland, and at least five went to work in Tunisia. Of those which returned to these shores, most went to the National Coal Board while others went to the Port of London Authority, Manchester Ship Canal and various steel works. It is known that some were still in service in 1983 and that others finished up in the hands of private enthusiasts. Construction of them as a class carried on until 1962.

ARMY PERSONNEL

Permanent personalities were few in number for the simple reason that the line was generally worked by the Operating Companies, Permanent Way Companies, Movement Control Units and Stores Companies who passed through on their varied careers. The permanent Technical Officer in charge was a Major C.A. Calder who later ran the Shropshire & Montgomery Railway for the War Department until closure. A delightful, mild-mannered man, he was an enthusiast first and foremost with a very sharp eye for any wrong moves. The Warrant Officer in charge was a 'Geordie' fellow named Joe Greener. After the war he ended his railway career in charge of the North Eastern Region Motive Power instruction train. CSM Hughes and Sgt Kipling were the signalling experts who gave lectures on military rules and regulations. These lectures were remarkable for their clarity and precision.

THE END OF THE LINE

The MMR was handed back to the LMSR on 1st January, 1945, and the LMS continued to work the civilian and military traffic on three shifts. However, as the military traffic fell away, so did the need for three shifts. In 1956 the 'Hours of Opening of Signal Boxes' book showed the following information:

> Chellaston Quarry: A wagon repair depot from 1 pm to 8.50 pm Mondays to Fridays.
> King's Newton: (Block post built by the Army) as required
> Melbourne: Monday to Friday – 7 am to 8.50 pm
> Worthington: Saturdays – 7 am to 2.50 pm

By 1960 the train service was five trains (SX) and four trains (SO). King's Newton depot was still open; Tonge & Breedon had closed in 1959, but Worthington and New Lount were still flourishing. A 20 mph speed limit had come into force from 4th October, 1947.

New Lount Colliery linked up with a colliery in the Coalville area in 1964 while ironstone supplies became exhausted at Worthington, consequently the end of the line as a viable entity was rapidly approaching. Station closures took effect as follows:

> Worthington – 4th May, 1964
> Melbourne – 5th July, 1965
> King's Newton ⎫
> Tonge & Breedon ⎬ 7th September, 1959
> New Lount (Ashby) – May 1955.

A private siding agreement with the Breedon and Cloud Hill Quarry Company kept the line open until 21st May, 1980, but before then a buffer stop at Worthington marked the end of the branch proper in 1968.

The LMSR did its best to keep the line going as an alternative route to the south for freight via Ashby, but it was the condition of Ticknall tunnel which really killed those hopes. Suffice to say that for those who served on it the line will for ever live in their memories.

The authors have to thank a former soldier who served on the Melbourne Military Railway for the foregoing information. He is railway enthusiast to the core, and we are greatly indebted to him. With true modesty he prefers that we acknowledge his permission to print the above information as being: 'From the personal notebook of a military railwayman, and provided by the Museum of Army Transport, Beverley.'

Appendix Two

The Melbourne Military Railway – 24/25 October, 1943
A visit by R.C. Riley

I was having a thoroughly dull time at Ranby Camp, Retford, and looking at the notice board daily to see if anything interesting turned up when, to my surprise, there was a request for volunteers for Royal Engineers Movement Control or Transportation units. I applied for RE Transportation at once and eventually came the time to go for interview. My Company Officer refused to send men for interview in army time so I left Retford behind a GC 'Jersey Lily' 4–4–2 bound for Sheffield on Saturday. (There were some compensations at Retford!) From Sheffield to Derby I travelled behind a 'Jubilee' and then phoned the unit for transport to Melbourne. By this time it was Saturday afternoon and when I was taken in to see Major Calder, RE, he said, 'I don't interview men on a Saturday afternoon. Take the liberty train to Derby and see me in the morning'. The liberty train duly left behind ex-MR class '3F' 0–6–0 No. 3473 but I was not on it. I was determined to look at the MMR.

The following locomotives were seen:

Dean Goods 0–6–0; WD 99 (ex-GWR 2528)
MR '1F' 0–6–0Ts: 1666, 1708, 1751, 1788, 1839, 1890
LNWR 0–6–0ST: 27477
WD 0–6–0ST: WD 5061
USA 0–6–0T: USA 1255, 1387, 1407/10, 1939/68/44/70/71
WD 0–6–0 Diesel: WD 4564 (Vulcan 4564/36)

All locomotives were Westinghouse fitted since the training was intended to prepare RE Sappers to work on European railways. The Westinghouse pumps on the MR 0–6–0Ts were stamped LTSR and had come off that company's 4–4–2Ts. No. 27477, an 1889 veteran was used to show potential fitters the basics of a steam engine. It was a very basic engine. The only action it is likely to have seen at Melbourne was to be taken to pieces and put together again. The coaches noted were ex-Caledonian Railway with six wheel bogies with which I was later to become familiar at Longmoor. The following morning, having no qualifications other than interest and enthusiasm, Major Calder decided I was just the sort of person Railway Operating required. And so back to Derby where on shed was a rebuilt ex-SECR class 'F1' 4–4–0 No. 1062 on loan (to remind me of home), a 'Jubilee' to Sheffield and a GCR 4–6–0 thence to Retford. My posting to Longmoor came six weeks later but that's another story!

On 20th April, 1960 I took part in the SLS 'Last train over the Shropshire & Montgomeryshire Railway', which line had been taken over by the Army to give further instruction in 1941. I was greatly interested to find Major Calder in charge and I reminded him of my interview at Melbourne, which he remembered, and he enquired about my subsequent postings. Sadly Major Calder was killed during the lifting of track on the S&MR.